YOU GOT
WHAT IT
TAKES

Library of Congress Control Number: 2015956058

ISBN: 978-1-63308-189-5 Print
        978-1-63308-190-1 Digital

Interior and Cover Design by R'tor John D. Maghuyop

1028 S Bishop Avenue, Dept. 178
Rolla, MO 65401
Printed in United States of America

BONITA QUINN

YOU GOT WHAT IT TAKES

CHALFANT ECKERT
PUBLISHING

TABLE OF CONTENTS

FOREWORD

What a great book! Bonita has captured the true essence of a life in Christ. We have within us the treasures and talents to accomplish all that God has for us to do for His Glory. God has a purpose for each of us, a mission we are on, and Bonita shares with us the reason we are here on earth, and helps us to look inside to find our true destiny. It doesn't matter where we come from or where we have been, it is where we are going in Christ that matters. We are equipped by God to accomplish our destiny through Christ who strengthens us. This book will encourage and direct you to find your purpose in God's Kingdom. Enjoy!

Dr. Kitty Bickford, DBS, CPC
Founder, Pasture Valley Children Missions and Benevolance

CHAPTER 1

ORIGINAL INTENT

"But we have this treasure in earthen vessels, that the
Excellency of the power may be of God, and not of us."
2 Corinthians 4:7

First of all, I would like to say to you that you are a treasure, and you have treasure inside of you and that makes you unique to the plan of God. Let's place our focus on "this treasure" in our earthen vessels. A treasure is something very valuable that is hidden or kept in a safe place. It is something that is very special and of vital importance, and has to be discovered in order to determine its true value.

God's original intent for you is housed within the treasure He intricately placed within you. You have to believe without a shadow of a doubt that you have greatness inside of you, waiting to be unleashed. You have something priceless inside of you that will unlock the promises of God in your life. Why did God call what is within you a treasure? God calls it a treasure, because it is extremely valuable for the kingdom of God to be manifested here on earth. It is your divine purpose and it will not only prosper the kingdom of God, but it will also prosper you.

Do not allow the enemy to devalue you with his wicked schemes and devices. It's as if your body is a container, and on the inside of it are rare jewels that are highly desired and diligently searched for in order to possess or to obtain the contents. Inside of you, you have special aspects no one else can do like you can. You have your own personal treasure that makes you unique and special. You have within in a custom-made treasure, which is to be used to achieve your God-given assignment on this earth.

I recently spoke to a retired colonel who explained to me how he spent so many years in the military, pursuing promotion and prestige in an effort to try to gain fulfillment within him, but, much to his dismay, none the accomplishments ever did the job. He said he was now on track with God in his life and is trying to re-invent himself. I told him I believed, contrarily, he was on a hunt to discover the treasure God placed inside of him. I told him, once you locate your treasure, you truly will find out from God what you were put here on earth to do. You will then find true fulfillment.

In response, the retired colonel recalled a story he heard about a man who was found in a restricted and heavily guarded place. When the armed guard approached the guy, he asked him two questions, "Who are you and what are you doing here? I thought to myself, wow that's it. Those are questions every human being should go to our Creator and ask Him.

Who am I and *what should I be doing here on earth?* Those are powerful questions that will change the course of our lives as we discover the answer to them. I must reemphasize the truth—you are treasured by God, not because of the treasure that is in you, but just because. God loves you without a cause. Allow the love of God to captivate you, as you understand the rejection, persecution, and suffering are part of the process.

Rejection has been a major part of my life, and I am going to share how it hurt, but how healing had to take place. After experiencing rejection, I developed tough skin, but I kept a soft and humble heart. We have to understand man's rejection has nothing to do with God's acceptance. The Lord is the only One ever who will never leave or forsake you, no matter the circumstances. You have something priceless inside of you, and this book is going to guide you along a path of discovery.

We all have something special pulsating on the inside of us, ready to be discovered and put into operation. God has a powerful purpose for you, which is divinely connected to your treasure and is meant to accomplish His original intent for your life. Actually, God's purpose and

His original intent for you can be used interchangeably. As we discover our individual original intent for being here, we will begin to encounter God in major ways. All of God's efforts toward you will begin to become evident and a beautiful process of discovery will begin within you. You will see things from God's perspective and hear things with a deeper perception than before.

The scripture in 2 Corinthians 4:8-9 says that:

"We are troubled on every side, yet not distressed; we are perplexed, but not in despair; Persecuted, but not forsaken; cast down, but not destroyed."

As you discover your treasure, agree with God about who you really are, and begin to be determined to accomplish God's will for your life, you automatically will encounter the troubles listed in these scriptures, but there is always a "but" behind all the trouble. The "but" in those scriptures were placed there to remind us God is for us and nothing will be able to stop His plan for your life, as you determine in your heart to be used by God.

You would think finding out your treasure and purpose in life would be so well accepted, but we have to realize there is a real devil out there and his name is Satan. He wants to destroy you and your purpose, because he is well aware you are God's instrument here on earth to be used to add to the Kingdom of God. Others will be able to discover their true purpose, as well, as we use our treasure for that purpose and on and on it goes until God's great commission is accomplished through us. Matthew 28:19a reads:

"Go ye therefore, and teach all nations."

I find it absolutely fascinating God didn't just put us here and tell us to accomplish His will, but He equipped us to do so, has given us grace, and is with us to help us in any way we need Him. God is well aware we are going to need Him tremendously and on many occasions desperately, every step of the way.

A treasure is usually something hidden from the surface and has to be searched for in order to obtain it. It is very valuable; therefore, it is hidden or kept in a safe place. Your treasure is hidden for divine purpose, on purpose. God wants us to search out our purpose so He can use the process we go through to search it out and to refine us that we may use our treasure appropriately. We should intentionally seek after the treasure inside of us so we will be able to use it for God's glory. You will love doing what you were created to do. It may look hard and tedious to others, but to you, it's the thing you are graced to do and you will love it. You will move from survival mode to a place of thriving in life.

You will begin to see yourself in a whole new way, as you are getting more and more familiar with that part of you. It will be the one thing God uses to bring you to contentment and peace within yourself. It will give you pleasure to allow God to use the treasure He has placed inside of you. I am so excited to help you to really start to examine yourself and spend time with just you and God so that God can guide you to your custom-made treasure. You are special and to be admired and God wants to bring that part of you out, so the world will see and glorify Him and also glean from the purpose He has created you. Sometimes we look at others and admire what they may be doing for the kingdom, but God is turning the spotlight on you and saying, "What about you? You have been given divine purpose as well."

Before God revealed to me how special I am and the great treasure I have inside of me, the enemy would plant self-loathing thoughts in my mind he wanted me to speak out over myself. The enemy used my own tongue against me. Because of a root of rejection in me; consequently, I agreed with the enemy and let him tell me lies about myself and I spoke the lies he was telling me until God intervened and set me free. Proverbs 18:20-21 explains this so vividly:

"A man's [moral] self shall be filled with the fruit of his mouth; and with the consequence of his words he must be satisfied [whether good or evil]. Death and life are in the power of the tongue, and they who indulge in it shall eat the fruit of it [for death or life]."

In order to overcome these insecurities, I had to denounce the things Satan was telling me to say, such as, "I hate myself. I'm nothing. I wish I was dead." Satan repeated these things over and over and over again, trying desperately to make me say what he was saying, so he could put me in a state of depression. I admit it worked until I understood what he was trying to do. After he couldn't get me to say those things, he would try to keep them on my mind by continuing to repeat them over and over again in my thoughts.

It was as if someone was sitting next to me, nudging me over and over, trying to get me to say it. I'm being very candid here, because I really want you to visualize just how the enemy tried to circumvent the great plan of God for my life. Every time I felt pain, made a mistake, or even got hurt, the enemy started to plant those negative thoughts in my mind trying to have me to speak them in first person to disguise the fact it was not my own thoughts, but the thoughts he planted in my mind to make me speak them into existence, giving life to them. The devil was desperately trying to use my thoughts against me because he knows that what you think about yourself is extremely important and vital to Gods divine purpose for your life.

Your thoughts must be tamed according to the will of God for your life. Proverbs 23:7a says:

"For as he thinks in his heart, so is he."

You have to change your thinking about yourself, as well as what you say about yourself. I had to begin to fill my mind with what God says about me, rather than entertain those things the devil tried to convince me to think. We actually become what we think. The enemy knows the power of the mind and that our actions will follow what we think about ourselves. We have to learn to think like God. The enemy will try to make his lies become your reality. Don't allow your mind to be a dumping ground for Satan's trash, but instead, make it the ground God uses to show you a vivid picture of yourself being used for His glory.

Use the imagination God gave you to let God take you on a journey to what He has for you and what He has for you to do. It may seem impossible and it may very well be in your own strength, but when God does it, all of a sudden, it becomes possible. Believe what God is showing you and do not allow the enemy to convince you otherwise. Although he will try very hard to convince you, you have to be determined and active in your persistence to think, say, and do the will of God for your life. I am reminded of a famous preacher who once said that when the enemy tries to fill your mind with negative or evil thoughts, stop and begin to fill your mind with the Word so the enemy will not have room to plant evil thoughts.

Your mind will be filled with the Word of God. Our thoughts are the root of our words and deeds. No matter what the enemy is trying to convince us to think about ourselves, God has in writing, so much He has to say about us in His Word. We must continually examine our thoughts in comparison to the light of God's Word, being always willing to submit our thoughts the His thoughts. In 2 Corinthians 10:4-5, this point is being explained. "Through careful strategy and cunning deceit, Satan attempts to set up "strongholds" in our minds." A stronghold is any argument or pretension that "sets itself up against the knowledge of God." Basically, it's an area that exalts itself in our minds, "pretending" to be bigger or having more power than our God. It makes us believe in our minds we are overpowered, or under its control. The mind is the battlefield. We must win the war in our minds in order to defeat the enemy. The scripture 2 Corinthians 10:3-5 holds the key to freedom from strongholds:

> "For though we live in the world, we do not wage war
> as the world does. The weapons we fight with are not the
> weapons of this world. On the contrary, they have divine
> power to demolish arguments and every pretension that
> sets itself up against the knowledge of God, and take
> captive every thought to make it obedient to Christ."

The enemy knows if he can influence our thinking, he can influence our behavior. Your mind dictates your behavior. Once you truly understand the importance of your mind and what is going on inside it, you will begin to control it by the authority God gives you and cast down any thing that exalts itself against the truth of God's Word. Wrong thinking will hold you in bondage. I know because I was in bondage to wrong thinking for years, but as I began practicing the Word of God and meditating on it, I got liberated and have been experiencing God in powerful ways in my life every since.

I am constantly using the Word of God to captivate my thinking and release me from the bondage of wrong thinking. Believe me, my education on this comes from my own failures of wrong thinking patterns. God showed me where I had been forfeiting my blessings, peace, and ability to bless others. Satan had gotten into my mind by planting his evil thoughts about me and he convinced me of his lies. I thank God for my liberation. Now, I am able to enlighten you, so you can become liberated too.

Nothing, absolutely nothing is more powerful than God. Say it out loud over and over again until it gets deep down into your spirit. Take authority and use the Word or God and Spirit-filled prayer as weapons to destroy strongholds. I began to ask God to give me His thoughts and give me His ways, because I understood as the Word says, they are higher than mine. The enemy was desperately trying to plant his low thoughts in my mind. This is illustrated in Isaiah 55:8-9, which says:

> *"For my thoughts are not your thoughts, neither are your ways My ways, says the Lord. For as the heavens are higher than the earth, so are My ways higher than your ways and My thoughts than your thoughts."*

Please carefully examine the thoughts you have of yourself.

If your thoughts are contrary to God's thoughts, then you must, with diligence and persistence, cast down those thoughts that are contrary to the word of God. Being able to have a true understanding of the Word of God well enough to compare your thoughts to the word is imperative. You have to begin to believe and have the mind of God, which is His Word. Do not lose the war of the mind to the enemy. The enemy knows what great treasure you have and he desperately tries to steal, kill, and destroy the plan God has for your treasure.

Wrong thoughts will make you miserable and the enemy knows it. I have learned by experience that when you are miserable you make others miserable around you also. Please inventory the thoughts you have about yourself, regularly and ask yourself this self-examining question, "What have I been thinking about myself"? This is especially true when you feel badly or have done something you are not proud of doing. Examine your thought life to determine the "why" behind what you are doing. I plead the blood of Jesus over my mind daily. I Corinthians 2:15-16 says:

> *"But he who is spiritual appraises all things, yet*
> *he himself is appraised by no one. For who has*
> *known the mind of the Lord, that he will instruct*
> *him? But we have the mind of Christ."*

I speak that I have the mind of Christ daily to cast down any thoughts the enemy is trying to plant.

God counteracted everything the enemy attempted to do in my life by showing me who I really was, and who I am today. God also began to show me how He has blessed me with this great treasure within. God began to build me up by taking the time to explain to me what He put inside of me and how special I am to Him. He built my vocabulary up about myself as I began to study and meditate on His word and saw what God had to say about me. I got to tell you, it made me smile over and over again. I blushed. I cried. I laughed. I surrendered myself to Him fully. I never knew those things were pertaining to me, until God led me over and over again to passages of scripture that convinced me that I was specially created for His divine purpose.

God gave me a renewed mindset about myself as He revealed to me who I really am in Him. Allow God to do the same for you. It will be an unforgettable experience and although it's a process, you will enjoy every moment you spend with your Maker. In the scripture Isaiah 6:1-2 says:

"Arise [from the depression and prostration in which circumstances have kept you-rise to a new life]! Shine (be radiant with the glory of the Lord), for your light has come, and the glory of the Lord has risen upon you. For behold, darkness shall cover the earth, and dense darkness [all] peoples, but the Lord shall arise upon you [O Jerusalem], and His glory shall be seen on you."

The glory of God will be seen on you and flow from within you. Men will see God's glory upon you and will want to get what you have. This is all a part of God's plan to draw all men to Him. When they come, let them know your testimony and who gives you that radiant shine. There is nothing or no one that can take that away from me now. I glow with the glory of the Lord. I also know that it's God's glory and not my own. God builds us up, but at the same time we must continually remind ourselves that the excellence is of God and not of us. We must keep things in perspective and humble ourselves under the hand of God as He gently guides us through to divine purpose.

Our words should be carefully orchestrated to fit God's purpose for our lives. I use the word "orchestrated" strategically, simply because what we speak have to be carefully chosen according to the plan God has for us to sculpt our way in Him.

"A word fitly spoken is like apples of gold in pictures of silver,"
Proverbs 25:11

As I meditated on that scripture, I pictured what looked like in my mind, and I smiled as I began to see how beautiful that would be. I thought about how placing the apples just right would make them shine brighter. Are you carefully orchestrating your words about yourself? It is vitally important that you do. That scripture says "fitly spoken" meaning your words have to fit the plan and design that God has for your life.

Your words have to fit who you really are. Your words have to be placed just right at the right time. Your words have to fit your original intent. Your thoughts and your words are to be carefully designed in order that your life will reflect God's purpose. I really want to deposit that deep within your spirit so you will understand its truth and be very careful what you think and say. Always, always, always be reminded of how thoughts and words about yourself are vital to your life. Let's examine what Mary, the mother of Jesus, said when she discovered her purpose in Luke 1:46-49:

> *"And Mary said, my soul magnifies and extols the Lord,*
> *And my spirit rejoices in God my Savior, For He has looked*
> *upon the low station and humiliation of His handmaiden.*
> *For behold, from now on all generations [of all ages] will*
> *call me blessed and declare me happy and to be envied!"*

For He who is Almighty has done great things for me-and holy is His name [to be venerated in His purity, majesty and glory]! In this passage of scripture, she was excited about her discovery of God's purpose for her life, but she also expressed in humility that she honored God and glorified Him. I think God was just as excited as she was. God had just told her that she was going to give birth to Jesus Christ, the Messiah, who they had been expecting to come forth for many years. What is it that God wants you to give birth to for His glory? Your treasure is there to give birth to something great and powerful. I want to encourage you and stir you up in your spirit.

Think of something on the inside of you that is buried deep and is pulsating, ready to be unleashed and as you speak life to it, it begins to grow and glow and flourish. It's radiant with great power to move things out of your way and in your way, for the sake of God's specially designed purpose. When God starts to help you to see yourself through His eyes, then your imagination will kick in and redirect your thinking to His thoughts of you. You will begin to see how big and valuable you and your purpose is to God. It will then become extremely important to you that you live what God is showing you.

Let it be a burning within you to accomplish His will. By getting into the Word of God, it will save your life and help you to live the abundant life God promises us. Without the Word of God, we are subject to anything the world has to offer. The word keeps us in peace and helps us to live free from the world's mindset, which cannot give us the life that is promised to us. Our mind has to be completely renewed by the Word of God.

> *"My son, give attention to my words; incline your ear*
> *to my sayings. Do not let them depart from your eyes;*
> *Keep them in the midst of your heart. For they are life*
> *to those who find them, and health to all their flesh"*
> Prov. 4:20-22

The treasure we have within is given for the glory of God. The treasure we have within is also for the edifying of the body of Christ and it illuminates God to the world around us. It has special purpose. It's not meant to be handled any old kind of way, although many people do. It's meant to be handled with care, why, because it is specially designed with greatness in mind. Your treasure should be treasured. I believe God is eager to disclose it to you. Begin to truly take the time to seek God. He wants to reveal the true treasure He has concealed. Proverbs 25:2 says:

> *"It is the glory of God to conceal a thing: but the*
> *honor of kings is to search out a matter."*

We are kings and priests to our God. Revelation 1:6 defines us as kings and priests:

> *"And has made us kings and priests unto God and his Father;*
> *to him be glory and dominion forever and ever. Amen."*

We have been placed here to be used in order for God's kingdom to be prevalent on this earth that we may win souls to Christ, by demonstrated His principles and way of living so that they may see God move through us as we display God's unconditional love towards them in the process. You have a treasure that God implanted inside of you that is the original intent for which you have been created. God's original intent for you is not predicated on what has happened to you in the past or not even what will happen to you, but it is completely orchestrated by God Almighty and nothing or no one can change it.

The original intent for which you were created is untouchable, and even you can't change what God designed you to be. My husband says, "When the enemy reminds you of your past to make you feel bad about yourself, tell him that he didn't go back far enough. He has to go back pass your past to your real past. If he really wants to remind you of your past, he needs to go back to the point where you were created before the foundation of the world." Psalm 139:13-15 says:

> "For You did form my inward parts; You did knit
> me together in my mother's womb. I will confess and praise
> You for You are fearful and wonderful and for the awful
> wonder of my birth! Wonderful are Your works, and that
> my soul knows right well. My frame was not hidden from
> You when I was being formed in secret [and] intricately and
> curiously wrought [as if embroidered with various colors] in
> the depths of the earth [a region of darkness and mystery]."

God's plan for our lives has been ordained in the spiritual realm from before the foundation of the world. It is a good plan that cannot be touched. Before we were even born, God had planned our days. Satan has been working very hard to terminate what God has planned for us and unfortunately he has succeeded in many lives. Let God reveal His plan to you and obey Him. Do not settle for anything less than what gives you the greatest joy. The problem is, so many people settle, but they don't seek. God has more for you. We can design a plan for our lives, but God has designed purpose for our lives.

Your plans for your life may change depending on circumstances, but God's purpose for you remains the same. It's still within you, intact. Sure we have things we have done also ourselves that we are not proud of doing. We all have made drastic mistakes. To me, a mistake is not as detrimental as the enemy makes it seem. I look at it as dross that has to be wiped away in order for greatness to be revealed. Things that reveal flaws that can be improved upon.

Mistakes are things that give you the ability to make changes that help to revamp your life and way of doing things. Proverbs 25:4 reads:

> *"Take away the dross from the silver, and there*
> *shall come forth a vessel for the finer."*

Come forth and shine for the glory of God. Although we have dross that needs to be wiped away, God's love for us will never change. His love is solid and comes with a lifetime guarantee. If anything breaks down, His love is right there to fix it. No charge. The price has already been paid. You are covered for life. Blessed be the name of the Lord!

I distinctly remember asking God one day how could He love me more than my mother loves me? After all, she is the one who gave birth to me. God said to me, "I didn't just give birth to you like your mother did, I created you. Your mother gave birth to you after you were conceived in her womb, but I created out of my love for you before you were conceived, then I strategically placed you in your mother's womb. I thought, wow that's awesome! I had never looked at it that way.

It gave me a better sense of worth and a deeper understanding of His love for me. God said, "There was much care involved in creating you." We must always remember that God has an original intent for us and find out from Him what it is and begin to speak it out. We see in Jeremiah 29:11 that:

> *"For I know the thoughts and plans that I have for you,*
> *says the Lord, thoughts and plans for welfare and peace*
> *and not for evil, to give you hope in your final outcome."*

Your treasure is directly tied to your purpose.

I am trying to explain to you that you have greatness inside of you needing to be discovered. I say greatness because God does not deal in mediocrity. If you are living a mediocre life, let me tell you, that is not what God has for you. He wants to reveal to you the greatness you were created for before the foundation of the world. God desires to allow you to discover the real you. It gives God good pleasure to show you to yourself, but we have to go to God to discover this awesome treasure within us and believe me, it is a great treasure. It's beyond what your natural mind can fathom.

That's why God has to reveal it to your spirit by His Spirit. The scripture, 1 Corinthians 2:9-10 says:

> *"But, on the contrary, as the Scripture says, what eye has not seen and ear has not heard and has not entered into the heart of man, [all that] God has prepared (made and keeps ready) for those who love Him [who hold Him in affectionate reverence, promptly obeying Him and gratefully recognizing the benefits He has bestowed]. Yet to us God has unveiled and revealed them by and through His Spirit, for the [Holy] Spirit searches diligently exploring and examining everything, even sounding the profound and bottomless things of God [the divine counsels and things hidden and beyond man's scrutiny]."*

As I began to meditate on this scripture, I got goose bumps inside and out when I realized God, Himself, has to reveal me to me through His Holy Spirit. Man can't touch what God has for you when you obey God. Glory to God! We all have treasures that the Holy Spirit will reveal to us as we obey God. The more we obey, the more He reveals. The more He reveals the more confidence we have in Him. The more confidence we have in Him, the more we step out on faith. The more we step out on faith, the more we begin to realize our destiny.

When I think of this, I think of times when I have bought something for my kids and I hid it from them for an appointed time. When the time came for me to reveal it to them, I'm just as excited or even more excited to give it to them than they are to receive it because I know what joy it's going to bring them. That's how God, our Father, feels. Once we know some of the things God has given to us in gifts, talents, and abilities, we must be careful how we use them. God's purpose is for us to show His love to whoever we help as we administer them. We should be aware God is really concerned with the "way" we use our gifts.

That's another reason why our treasure is hidden, because as we search it out, God is working on our character. God is working on purifying our motives. God is working on us, in general, so we may carry His treasure well and honor Him as we use it. Please take the time to really get into the presence of God so that God can begin to reveal those things to you. God wants to spend quality time with you. God wants to show you the greatness within you. Although God could actually make you sit down and get into His presence, He doesn't do that. God wants to gently woo you into His presence and reveal these things to you. God will also work diligently on your character in order to help you to understand how you are to use your gifts or treasure. You see, all that dross that God removes is just a part of you being processed for greater use. So that you will use your treasure in love.

The 12th chapter of 2 Corinthians talks about us being many members, but one body. Then it goes on to talk about our gifts. At the end of the chapter, verse 31 reads:

"But earnestly desire and zealously cultivate the greatest and best gifts and graces (higher gifts and the choicest graces). And yet I will show you a still more excellent way [one that is better by far and the highest of them all—LOVE]."

What that means is everything else is great to have, but what far surpasses them all is love. Love is the highest of them all. For example, it's as if you were a runner competing in a race and many of the other runners are closely running against each other as far as speed is concerned, but then you far outrun them all. There is this big gap between you and the other runners, and you are way ahead of the others.

The gap is wide, and there is no catching up. That is love in comparison to any gifts we may possess. It's the greatest gift that we could ever give. There is no comparison. Love is the ultimate of them all. It outshines them all and it makes them all shine brighter when they are used in conjunction with love. God doesn't even want us to give any other gift without it being given with the love of Christ. You must be motivated by love or God will not get the glory. We are blessed with gifts to be a blessing. That's why I have no problem asking God to bless me. I know what it's all about. We cannot bless others if we are not blessed.

God promised Abram in Genesis 12:2:

> *"And I will make you a great nation, And I will bless you,*
> *And make your name great; And so you shall be a blessing."*

Notice the word "so" in the verse. God specified that He was blessing Abram "so" he would be a blessing. God was making Abram's name great for His glory, not for Abrams glory. I believe every gift, talent, and ability we have been blessed with is to be used out of and with love to glorify God as He uses us to help mankind. Now that I'm a changed person, I am driven by being able to help someone, anyone, and everyone I can.

Paul continues on in Chapter 13 to teach about how to use our gifts and talents. Paul explains very specifically without love it is of no use to the kingdom of God. Love must be intertwined with all the gifts we use and love must be the ultimate reason why you use your gifts. Allow your work for the Lord to be love motivated. The next verse, Verse 13, says:

> *"And now abide faith, hope, love, these three,*
> *but the greatest of these is love."*

Please do not allow yourself to be so engulfed with your gift that you neglect to be motivated by love as you use it. As a matter of fact, if you really think about it, you don't use your gift, but, your gift uses you, when you are led by the Spirit of God. If you are just a vessel, then you go around doing what the Holy Spirit dictates from your gift. When your gift uses you, you are led by the Holy Spirit. I have come in contact with those who use their gift/gifts, but not with or motivated by love.

Believe me, the truth of the matter is that love is the only reason God gave it to you. God gave you gifts in order that you may be used to love mankind as you use them. God was motivated by love when He gave it to you and God expects us to share what He has blessed us with as a blessing to others. But the enemy tries to throw you off track with different things that happen to you. Know he is already defeated. Jesus defeated him with the power of God. You can get ahead of his tactics, as you are being led by the Holy Spirit. There is supernatural power available to us when we obey God. The supernatural, as a matter of fact is meant to trump anything the enemy throws at us. The supernatural enables us to boast about our God. The supernatural is just that, "Super!" natural and when God works through us in the supernatural, His glory is personified through us.

Have you ever experienced how it seems some people have so much to offer the kingdom, but they're puffed up or they try to do the will of God, but they keep getting off track somehow? They are up one minute and down the next minute. They're unstable, fickle, or sometimes just downright mean. Perhaps this may reflect some of your own behaviors.

I asked God one day, "Why is that? Why do people act that way?"

God then began to explain to me why. What a journey that was.

He explained to me, "There are countless things going on inside of them that they have hidden."

"What are those things, God"? I asked.

He said, "Rape, incest, adultery, verbal abuse, physical abuse, and so much more that they have suppressed because of the hurt and pain that they just cannot seem to get pass because they have not truly surrendered them to Me. During those times, they are unstable, all of that stuff begins to bleed out. It's got to go somewhere. It's no small matter. It's all so strong within them, it spills out in some way. It hit them—so hard they can only suppress it for so long. Many of them cannot even explain their own behavior."

Perhaps this is you. Perhaps things have happened to you that come up every now and then that make you angry, unstable, and frustrated, which makes you stop and veer off course, slow down and feel somewhat depressed or even go into full depression or maybe feel down about yourself and you cannot explain why you feel that way at times. Those exact things may not come to mind, but subconsciously they hinder you and your walk with God.

God told me to be careful about how you see people behave, because there is a reason you may not see or be aware of, that caused this behavior. God continued on to say they cannot truly glorify me with all that going on inside of them. People need to be honest about what has happened to them. God wants us to truly come clean and admit what has happened to us so we can understand these behavior changes that we are experiencing. You have to expose the enemy and not keep allowing him to jerk you back anytime he gets ready, which is usually when you are beginning to excel and move forward.

The enemy begins to bring up your past because he sees that your future is going to make his bottomless pit less crowded. God predestined you for something great and has a powerful destiny that He has planned for you. Ephesians 2:8-10 says:

> *"For by grace you have been saved through faith. And this is not your own doing; it is the gift of God, not a result of works, so that no one may boast. For we are his workmanship, created in Christ Jesus for good works, which God prepared beforehand, that we should walk in them."*

That is what the enemy is after, your treasure because he knows how valuable it is to the kingdom of God. That is why it is called your "treasure." God has given you great treasures that are hidden that the enemy cannot touch, so the enemy desires to use you and then sift you as wheat. He wants to use you and then destroy you. Jesus communicated this to Peter as He began to tell Peter that he would deny him in Luke 22:31. He said:

> *"And the Lord said, Simon, Simon, behold Satan hath desired to have you, that he may sift you as wheat."*

His ultimate goal is to destroy you in order that you may not fulfill God's purpose for creating you. God's purpose for your life is not for you, it's for mankind. The enemy wants to gain control any time he gets ready, that's why he strategically waits for the most opportunistic time to pull you back and keep you down and out. Therefore, by the grace of God, this book is specifically sent by God to expose him and his tactics. The power of God has enabled us to house such treasures within, that it will take God Himself to reveal them to us so that the glory of the power will be of God and not of us. We will not be able to take the credit for the things God has placed inside of us because some of the treasure inside can only be found through Him. I must say, there is no way I would have thought to be writing books, especially Christian books that God has given me to help people if I had not allowed God to reveal this to me.

There are things you can do as well. There are areas that you have not even tapped into that God, your Creator, is waiting to reveal to you. Many things that people have done through Christ, I often hear them say, "I didn't even know I could do it," which is absolutely correct. Some things are hidden for the simple reason that the power may be of God, and not of us. Over and over again God reveals Himself through the wonders of His works through us. Over and over again we have to rely on the grace of God to accomplish the wonders of His work. Over and over again when you fashion in your mind to be obedient to God, He will admonish you to do impossible things. I still find it amazing the things God gets done through ordinary people like you and me.

Although we have great treasure within, we are very often, being held down by those things that the enemy uses in order that your treasure will not be revealed to you or to the world. Do not allow the enemy to remind you of your past to belittle you and make you stay in that stuck place. You give him the right to do it as you continue to hide and shuffle under the rug those things that were so detrimental to you that caused so much pain. Although you think you got over it, every now and again you are reminded just to keep you feeling ashamed enough to hide it all. You really give the enemy hidden power over you whenever you do that.

You also protect it from being exposed. I admonish you to please get help from a trusted source. Get to the altar and allow God to take it all from you and deliver you from it. Also, follow up with your spiritual leader in order to get the support you need through the journey to healing and forgiveness or rather forgiveness then healing because you must forgive first so that your complete healing will take place.

I'm reminded of a person I know who was very gifted in so many areas. She was going through so much at home and at work. She could not find a church good enough for her because of her critical spirit. She was just an unhappy person on the inside, but on the outside she seemed so jovial, but she could be very mean at times and very harsh to others without even blinking an eye. People said it was her personality, but I could not agree. God kept telling me that she is hiding something and she needs healing or she will continue to hurt inside and just be unhappy, harsh and hard-hearted. She didn't care if she hurt people she just wanted to get her point across. She did not care how she made people feel.

At times, the way she spoke to others was nothing short of disrespect. She had grown callous to the feelings of others. The hurt inside made her begin to hurt others and not care about how they felt. If she felt justified, she would tear you to pieces. I began to see, even when people gave her a complement, it was hard for her to really receive the complement. Sure, you definitely want to give God all glory, but God began to show me in those times the enemy would say things to her to make her feel bad about herself. Right away, the enemy started to remind her of her past and condemn her or belittle her. She had terrible mood swings.

She had so much hurt, resentment, and bitterness going on inside of her that she broke down one time at home and began to pray. She asked God, "What hinders me? Why do I continue to bounce up and down like this?"

She felt herself begin to gag. She immediately had to run to the bathroom to regurgitate (vomit). At that moment, she heard the doorbell ring. She finished and wiped her mouth and went to the door. It was me at the door, as I was on my way home one day, and God told me to stop by her house and that she needed me. Well, I had not seen or spoken to her in a long time so I started telling God that and stopping by would not be a good idea. You know how we do to reason our way out of doing the will of God when it is going to make us uncomfortable.

As if God does not know why we are trying to get out of it and what the outcome would be. I proceeded to reason with God, trying to get out of it, but I found myself pulling up in her driveway believe it or not.

I just got out of the car in obedience. I felt so awkward, but I was sure it was God.

I rang the doorbell and she came to the door in tears. It was as if God had told her I was coming because she didn't seem surprised to see me at all, instead she hugged me. In tears, she showed me to my seat and told me what she had just experienced. Then she asked me, what did it mean? God revealed to me that she had so much bitterness inside of her that she needed to come to terms with so He could deal with it and take the bitterness and pain away as she forgave all the people that hurt her.

There were a lot of bitter roots. God had given me a word for her to let go of the past incidents that happened to her and forgive those who did it all. Then her healing would take place as she let Him minister His divine comfort to her. She had so much resentment inside of her towards her father and so many people, to include her husband that she could not truly commit to the things of God because of all the bitterness. All of her good treasure that was meant for the edification of the body and the glory of God was buried under all the rubbish that happened to her in the past. Her father had forced her to get an abortion at a young age. She had been verbally, mentally, and physically abused by her husband, throughout their marriage. He also had cheated on her countless times.

On the surface, it looked like she flat had it going on. I mean, materially, she had all she could ask for and more—a beautiful home, nice car, and a six-figure income, but she was still so very bitter and harsh hearted at times. Everyone knew not to cross her or she would let you have it. Those things that happened to her in the past, was affecting her walk with Christ. It was a whole lot of past hurts keeping her in bondage in this vicious cycle.

Maybe you have harbored so much inside that it seeps on to others. Maybe you are literally trying to be who God created you to be, but that stuff keeps coming up. You don't know why you get so angry over the smallest of things. You are not even conscious of it, but it's there and it keeps you down or on a roller coaster. Satan keeps reminding you of it and subconsciously you are affected by it. You see, your treasure is still there, some you know about, but some you won't know are there until you are free. What the enemy takes you to, is what happened to you in the past, the pain and suffering it caused you. He doesn't take you back to God's original intent. That would be detrimental to his plan. God's original intent for you is hanging in the balance, waiting to be discovered and explored. Make no mistake about it, your life has powerful purpose. You need to be in hot pursuit of it in order to discover it, use it and let destiny take place in your life for the glory of God.

Believe God loves you deeply and will bring it to pass. Now you know the "why" that explains it all. God's excellence is on the inside of you waiting to be discovered to help you excel. God's original intent for you is to excel to the point that you are driven to help others with what He has put on the inside of you. Your driving force should ultimately be God's original intent for your life, but the enemy tries to intercept the plan and have you running in the wrong direction by planting evil in your life. 2 Corinthians 2:11 tells us:

> *"Lest Satan should get an advantage of us:*
> *for we are not ignorant of his devices."*

Don't let him win. You have more power than you can ever imagine, in Christ. I know you cannot help what others have done to you, but you can help how you allow it to affect your life. You have to be determined to allow the Word of God to gear you in the right direction. The Holy Spirit is a person and He comes along to guide you into all truth. Let The Holy Spirit show you the truth about you.

Jesus told His disciples in John 16:13:

> *"But when He, the Spirit of Truth (Truth-giving Spirit)*
> *comes, He will guide you into all the Truth (the whole,*
> *full Truth). For He will not speak His own message [on His*
> *own authority]; but He will tell whatever He hears [from*
> *the Father; He will give the message that has been given*
> *to Him], and He will announce and declare to you the*
> *things that are to come [that will happen in the future]."*

The Holy Spirit gives you dreams and visions of yourself doing what most excites you and is far beyond anything you can accomplish on your own without God. You should be on a mission to agree with God and pursue it. Now I never thought I'd be writing books or speaking to crowds of people about the goodness of God, but little by little God revealed my treasure to me, and I have been in hot pursuit of glorifying Him with it every since.

CHAPTER 2

BEING SPIRITUALLY HEALTHY

Spiritual health keeps us strong in multiple areas in a balanced way. We need the wisdom of God to balance our lives and keep things in proper perspective. I believe that once we receive the love of Christ, everything else will start to get prioritized around that truth. I am now able to really and truly say that God is my source and deliverer in all I go through. He's a superb teacher who allows life itself to teach us as He gently guides us through it. Be assured, He's always there. The problem is, we don't always acknowledge His presence.

His presence is ultimately the absolute best place to be and, as we acknowledge Him, wow, what joy it brings. God's presence brings such rest, serenity, peace, security, knowledge, insight, and joy unspeakable just to name a few. The list goes on and on. Whatever we need God to be at that moment, we can find in His presence. We learn so much in His presence. Powerful spiritual health begins to occur and balance is inevitable. Every part of your being is better when you are in His presence. I sometimes feel like I'm in this cloud that whisks me away into a place of perfect tranquility. I don't have to do anything, just be. You have got to experience it, there is nothing like it. Oh, taste and see that the Lord is good.

I often strongly sense the presence of God so much so that it gives me great joy unspeakable. I am elated that God chose me at that particular moment to touch when so many others have shunned me and walked away from me without remorse. God lets me know right at that very moment that He is more than enough. Experiencing God that way is completely fulfilling and breathtaking to me, it's amazing. Then there are times when I just want to worship God and love on God and during those times I am reminded that God loved me first. I'm reminded of all God did for me at Calvary and even before Calvary. I have times when I just want to thank Him all day long and I do. Can you just sense His love even as I explain my experiences with Him? I must say, I know how you feel because I'm feeling it right now. Saying, "God is so good" has taken on a brand new meaning for me. I feel a warm sensation going through me as I say it now. It makes you think of it and smile just to be smiling. I want you to really grasp that love through this writing He has given us. I feel compelled to tell you that really and truly, it's Him. He's the one who wants you to experience receiving His love in a whole new and fulfilling way. God wants you to experience His love in a way that will allow you to win in everything, everywhere, all the time.

No matter who you are, what you've done, or where you are in life, God loves you. Romans 8:35 says:

> *"Who can separate us from the love of*
> *Christ shall tribulation or distress, or persecution,*
> *or famine, or nakedness, or peril, or sword?"*

There is absolutely nothing you or anyone else can do about that great love. What an amazing truth. Glory to God! Once I truly began to realize that God loves me no matter what, I was able to be at rest with everything else that went on in my life. His love keeps us grounded. The love of God is our security when life makes us feel insecure. God's love will transform your thinking into His thinking and your ways into His ways. If you can't find a way, He will show you His way. Embrace this great love and your life will change forever. You will have confidence that man alone cannot give you. Do you remember the day when you fell in love or met that person that you knew you would spend the rest of your life with or just falling in love?

That is no comparison to God's love for us. I want to try and help you get an idea of how I felt when God told me He loved me and I received it. I was standing in front my fireplace, trying to get warm after being in my prayer room meditating. I was still thinking about some things that I needed to take care of, but still engaged in His presence and I heard Him say to me, "I love you." He whispered it in my ear gently and lovingly. Like a warm wind that was so compelling. I was absolutely blown away at that moment. I could feel my body warm up on the inside. You see, the fireplace was good for the outside, but it took God to saturate the inside of me with His love. I felt a tingle going down my neck and spine. It was exactly what I needed to hear and it felt immensely refreshing. It felt like a breath of fresh air blowing gently across my face. I began to feel completely warm inside. I felt chills all over my body. I get chills even now when I think about it. I started to cry and praise and worship Him all at the same time. I danced and shouted all over the room. I remember that moment as if it were yesterday. I will never forget it because I truly believe that was the moment I received His love fully.

Once you receive God's love, it will begin to shield you and protect you. It will give you the joy you need for strength. You won't be so worried about things and people. You will begin to have an inner peace that satisfies the soul. There will definitely be some tough times that you will encounter, but knowing about that deep love will make you run when you get weary and walk when you feel faint. It will help you to see things in a different way. You will begin to know that whatever goes on, whatever the disappointments may be, God will make sure you are going to win in spite of it all because He loves you and has your absolute best interest at heart. We have to stop ourselves at times to really meditate on that so we won't let things and issues in life take us down a road of despair, and discontentment.

As I express this to you, I am reflecting on many times praying to God that He would fill me with the fullness of Him. I believe God did it that day. I literally felt God's touch like never before. I was able to hear Him so clearly. It was like He was standing right in front of me. I was able to understand that great love He had given me in a brand new way. I am now able to be at peace in a whole new way. I am now able to share in His passion to love His people. I could sense His presence like never before. God let me see Him like I had never seen Him before. I knew my purpose would be fulfilled at that moment. I'm not afraid of what may or may not happen anymore. God made me better in that moment. I longed to be everything, all at once that He desired me to be. I became desperate to help people and love people. God will give you zeal and compassion for mankind. It's as if, God planted His love for others inside me. God then said to me, "You can do all things through Christ who strengthens you." He was telling me that I would have many challenges to come, but through knowing and receiving His love for me that I could do all things through Him.

My strength would come from knowing and receiving His love. Everything I would be faced with from that point on was possible because of His love and the finished work that Jesus accomplished for me on the cross. You can face impossible situations with Him and He will make them entirely possible for you. No, I didn't know what the challenges were, but I completely grasped and understood more vividly that He loves me dearly and compassionately and every impossible situation I would face was entirely possible because of that love. I was captivated by that love and I have not been the same since that day. After that experience, when I say the name of Jesus, it is with an assurance that He loves me and His love strengthens my faith and it is truly all I need to know to accomplish His will. That was an unforgettable encounter.

> *"For I am persuaded beyond doubt (am sure) that*
> *neither death nor life, nor angels nor principalities,*
> *nor things impending and threatening nor things to*
> *come, nor powers, nor height nor depth, nor anything*
> *else in all creation will be able to separate us from the*
> *love of God which is in Christ Jesus our Lord"*
> Romans 8:38-39

You can be sure that through God's unfailing love, you can experience life with absolute victory through immeasurable adversity.

You see, it's times like that, that really makes the difference in my life to help me to keep pressing and standing fast in the most difficult of circumstances. Praying and meditating on the love of God through difficult times equips you with whatever you need to make it through, during the many challenges life has to offer. I began to reflect on the finished work of Jesus. How He made our victories possible. How we are already victorious before any challenge or difficult situation begins. We are in a position of victory because of what He accomplished on the cross. Jesus is everything for us whenever we need Him. I am totally and completely convinced without a shadow of a doubt that He is my everything, and He will show up in everything in my life. Every time I call on Jesus, He will answer. He will never ignore my pain or my struggle. Jeremiah 33: 3 says:

> *"Call to me, and I will answer you, and show you*
> *great and mighty things, which you do not know."*

All we have to do is call Him.

You must truly believe that. We have to truly rest in that truth. That has to set up residence in your spirit. As a matter of fact, saying the name of Jesus, backs the enemy up and defeats whatever plan he tries to bring to pass in our lives, but you have to be totally convinced of that love when you call His name. The love of God will empower you mentally, physically, and spiritually. There is absolutely nothing that you will not be able to accomplish through God's love. That is why God told me that day that I can do all things through Christ, which strengthens me. It is because I know God loves me. That truth is what gives me the ability and might to do all the things God tells me to do. Get excited about God's love. Engage yourself in activities that reflect God's love. Find ways to give out God's love. God's love will compel you to help somebody, anybody, whoever needs help. You will be eager to give help to whomever you can. No job is too small or large when it comes to kingdom work.

God is the originator of teams. Jesus and the Disciples were a team that God put together. Think of yourself as a part of this great team, the

Kingdom's work team, orchestrated carefully by God to carry out His plan on earth. That's what His unconditional love is all about. Receiving that great love so you can help mankind. You may not even remotely desire to help others now, but after you receive God's love for yourself, you will be compelled to perpetuate that great love in some way to others. I smile now on many occasions not because everything is always perfect, but because I have received God's love for me.

Take a moment right now and meditate on the love of the Father. Receive His love now and let it resonate in your spirit. Drink it down like a cool drink that hits the spot because that's what God's love does, it hits the spot. I can truly say that although it didn't stop the bad news from coming, it stopped me from allowing that bad news to break me. His love is a shield for us. It will take the hits for you and make you stronger. God's love is perfect and in that perfected love, you can take it. His love will grow you in strength, power, and faith. My faith was no longer hindered by circumstances when I received the love of God because I began to really trust God completely. I can sense the grace of God come upon me when I am faced with difficulties. God's grace is an extension of the perfected love He has for us. God's grace will abound for us as we abound in good works.

The more good works we set out to accomplish, the more God's grace steps in to meet us at any point of need.

> *"And God is able to make all grace abound (every favor*
> *and earthly blessing) come to you in abundance, so*
> *that you may always and under all circumstances and*
> *whatever the need be self-sufficient [possessing enough to*
> *require no aid or support and furnished in abundance*
> *for every good work and charitable donation]"*
> 2 Corinthians 9:8

Others may not be able to see what God has told you to do because they are looking at you and not at the grace that God has given you to complete the work, but God's grace is the secret weapon in your life that will make your ordinary become extremely extraordinary. The mere fact that you can do it, is extraordinary. You will be able to get more done through God's grace than you would with a whole lot of help in the natural. Sometimes you just have to step away and regroup in order to let God show you what to do and how to do it because people will try to help, but their limited thinking also limits you. People will help you, but God will reveal the ones that will help to you. As God gives grace for you, it becomes easier to flow according to the will of God. People will be at awe at what you do for God, but you will know where your help comes from.

You will know it was only by the grace of God. That keeps me humble because I am reminded so often of how I would not be able to do what God says without God. There is absolutely no way unless He does it through me. This is where God gets the glory. God must get the glory in order for us to lead or point people to God and not us. This is where you have an opportunity to testify of God making you adequate when you know you are completely inadequate for whatever good work you are doing for God. Our lives will then glorify God and the excellence of our treasure will be of Him and not of us.

I'm reminded of the Samaritan woman and how it was just an ordinary day for her, but she encountered Jesus that day in such a way that changed her life forever. You see, Jesus knew of her lifestyle, yet it didn't stop Him from loving her and wanting to help her. Jesus was aware of her present circumstances, but it didn't stop Him from communing with her. Sometimes people think that they have done so much sin and because of their present circumstance that God doesn't love them and does not want to help them, but that could not be farther from the truth. Could this be you? Do you feel sometimes that you want God, but maybe because of your lifestyle that He doesn't want you? Do not believe the lie that Satan convinces so many people to believe. God desperately wants to help any and everyone who will admit they need His perfect love. I know I needed His perfect love. I needed that unconditional love to help me and open my eyes to who I really am in Him. The Samaritan woman needed the exact same thing. Jesus knew her story, but it never stopped Him from sharing His love with her. Jesus was on Divine assignment to rescue her. John 4:4 says:

"And He must needs go through Samaria."

Even though Jesus' disciples went on to another city, He was destined to go through Samaria. Jesus understood His assignment.

As Jesus sat at the well, the Samaritan woman came at a time when she possibly thought no one would be there because of her present lifestyle. She was probably shunned by the religious sect. You know the spotless saints that are so holy they would never be caught talking to such a woman. Well, Jesus did just that out in the open where the world could see. He boldly went, on purpose, to help her. When Jesus asked her for a drink in John 4:9:

> *"The Samaritan woman said to Him, How is it that You,*
> *being a Jew, ask me, a Samaritan [and a] woman, for a*
> *drink? For the Jews have nothing to do with the Samaritans."*

Here is absolute proof that religious people are missing the very ones Jesus came to save. He didn't come to save the saved. He came to save the lost.

The Samaritan woman obviously had some dealings with the religious sect. I know I have, whew, I thank God for my relationship with Him that blew religion to pieces and met me at my point of need with no strings attached. All I had to do was to accept Him. That's all anyone has to do. The Samaritan woman had to be met by Jesus at her point of need as well. Jesus said He needed to go through Samaria. Jesus was purposed to meet up with her at that point. Jesus was not concerned with what the crowd thought. Jesus went alone. According to John 4:8:

> *"For His disciples had gone off into the town to buy food."*

Sometimes you have to hear from God and do what He is telling you to do regardless of what everyone else has on their agenda. God's agenda is what matters. There are lives at stake. Jesus had to save a life and He was obedient. His love crossed all barriers that had been set up by the Jews or tradition. The Samaritan woman was still stuck in tradition that tried to stop the flow of the power of love that was about to captivate her and change her life forever. Jesus didn't let that stop Him. Jesus pressed in to what He was sent there to do.

We must do the same. Do not allow what someone may be thinking to stop you from allowing God to use you as a conduit for His unconditional love. Keep loving no matter what. Jesus had to meet her right where she was and elevate her thinking to where it needed to be and that is how we should be. She had no clue of what she was about to encounter. We should elevate our own thinking and God will use us to do the same for others. Jesus simply walked with her step by step in order to change her mindset to believe who He was and that He knew all about her, but still loved her sincerely and deeply with no strings attached. As Jesus spoke with her, she began to understand what Jesus was saying and in John 4:25:

> *"The woman said to Him, I know that Messiah is coming, He Who is called the Christ (the Anointed One); and when He arrives, He will tell us everything we need to know and make it clear to us."*

Jesus reminded her of what she had been taught about Him. Jesus tapped in to her own knowledge and convinced her of who He was.

> *"Jesus said to her, I Who now speak with you am He"*
> John 4:26

Now this is where the power of God hit her so strong that she dropped everything and shouted. Although it didn't say she shouted, can you imagine the power she received at that moment and because of her excitement she ran back into town telling everyone with enthusiasm and a new found freedom. She had to be extremely excited. She was met at her point of need by the Messiah. Have you ever been there? I have definitely been there. She didn't care who heard her. She was testifying of her encounter with Jesus. That's what God wants. God wants us to share our encounters with Him with others, so that He will be glorified and win the lost. John 4:28-30 reports:

> *"Then the woman left her water jar and went away to the town. And she began telling the people, Come, see a Man Who has told me everything that I ever did! Can this be [is not this] the Christ? [Must not this be the Messiah, the Anointed One?] So the people left the town and set out to go to Him."*

I can imagine the town's people who knew her probably thought to themselves, if He can help you, knowing your reputation, surely He can help me. The Samaritan woman was captivated by His unconditional love and acceptance.

That's basically all Jesus did, He showed her some true and genuine love as He poured that living water inside her. She ran and shouted to the whole town what she had just experienced through the love of Christ. She was not ashamed of herself anymore and she did not care what people thought of her. She just took off on a mission to glorify God without delay. The time was ripe and ready and she flew to her purpose and the people left the town and set out to encounter Jesus, the true and living water for themselves. Jesus told her in John 4:14:

> *"But whoever takes a drink of the water that I will give him shall never, no never, be thirsty any more. But the water that I will give him shall become a spring of water welling up (flowing, bubbling) [continually] within him unto (into, for) eternal life."*

I believe the Samaritan woman felt that water welling up, flowing, and bubbling within her spirit as it satisfied every part of her being.

That's that living water. It is absolutely remarkable. This is not just words on a page. This actually happened. Can you just imagine it? I can sense His presence now myself. I think I'm going to take a pause here and shout! Won't you join me! Glory to God! Psalms 81:10 says:

"I am the Lord your God, Who brought you up out of the land of Egypt. Open your mouth wide and I will fill it."

The Samaritan woman opened herself up as she listened to Jesus to receive from Him and Jesus poured Himself in her, the living water and new life into her spirit. As we open ourselves up to God there is endless possibilities of experiencing the presence of God that we can receive. Open yourself up fully to God and God will fill you up with Him. Ephesians 3:19 states:

"[That you may really come] to know [practically, through experience for yourselves] the love of Christ, which far surpasses mere knowledge [without experience]; that you may be filled [through all your being] unto all the fullness of God [may have the richest measure of the divine Presence, and become a body wholly filled and flooded with God Himself]!"

The Samaritan woman had knowledge of him, but no experience. She knew of the Messiah, but her experience with Christ is what made the difference. Open yourself up to experience God in His fullness. You will not be disappointed. Instead, you will be completely filled with Him and whatever you need from Him. You can have a brand new experience with God everyday if you let Him. God is multifaceted. He is colorful, vibrant, clean, pure, sweet, compelling, resourceful, powerful, and so much more.

We should live to glorify God in all that we do. Jesus should be the center of everything we do throughout life. As we keep Him where He should be in our lives, it keeps everything else in perspective. He will keep our heart right concerning things that will tend to sway us in a compromising position. There will be no compromise in us because the Holy Spirit will remind us of God's ways verses worldly or fleshly ways. The more we want to put God in certain places and not in everything, the more the enemy can have an influence in our lives. The enemy looks for places he can use to defeat you. He wants to find where you are weak and make you entertain him. That is enough to get me determined to not allow him any room to move in my life. Thus, that being said, I know I have to stay connected to Jesus. We should always remember to stay plugged in to our Savior. He is our Source of victory.

"For in Him we live, and move, and have our being"
Acts 17:28a

I like to see myself in a place that is set aside in God. I believe that God wants us to see Him as a place to live, not just a go to every now and then, but to live.

*"He that dwells in the secret place of the Most High
shall remain stable and fixed under the shadow of the
Almighty [whose powers no foe can withstand]"*
Psalms 91:1

That is a place of total victory, a place that you can count on in a pinch, a place that conditions you for victory, a place where God allows you to be yourself and God to be Himself in your situation.

You can find it everywhere you go. You don't have to even still away naturally. You can start talking to God anywhere and enter into that place. Amazingly enough you can find it in the most difficult circumstances. No matter where you are, God has a way of showing that He is there. Paul so many times found himself in impossible situations because he preached and testified of his deliverance. Paul's life was threatened innumerably, but God was always there to keep him.

*"For He will give His angels [special] charge over
you to accompany and defend and preserve you
in all your ways [of obedience and service]"*
Psalms 91:11

Paul knew he was a kept man. Paul was convinced that he was sent by God, and no one could stop the plan of God for his life. That is the attitude we must also take in order to be effective for the kingdom because persecutions will come. Men will hate you for no reason. People will try to convince you that you are not doing the will of God. The more you press in, the harder you will have to stay focused in on the power of God to help you. John 16:33 says:

> *"I have told you these things, so that in Me you may have [perfect] peace and confidence. In the world you have tribulation and trials and distress and frustration; but be of good cheer [take courage; be confident, certain, undaunted]! For I have overcome the world." [I have deprived it of power to harm you and have conquered it for you.]*

Meditate on that scripture during those tough times. Speak it out so your faith in that truth will override adversity. There are things that we have to go through as saints of God that will definitely hurt us, but we have to redeem the time like Paul did and allow God to grace us through what we are going through in order that others will see God working through us, no matter what. Paul found himself many times in situations that could have rendered complaining, but he had a made up mind to decrease, that it was no longer him that lived, but Christ that lived in him. Paul writes in Galatians 2:20:

> *"I am crucified with Christ nevertheless I live; yet not I, but Christ lives in me: and the life which I now live in the flesh I live by the faith of the Son of God, who loved me, and gave Himself for me."*

Paul was convinced of the love of Christ, and he proved it by stepping out on faith countless times. Without Paul's faith in God's love for him, he would not have written a third of the bible for us to live by today. Most of which, was written in prison. For example, while Paul was in prison, he wrote and encouraged the saints on the outside. Yes, he could have complained, but he chose to abstain from complaining and encourage others instead. Let's read Colossians 4:2-6:

"Continue earnestly in prayer, being vigilant in it with thanksgiving; meanwhile praying also for us, that God would open to us a door for the word, to speak the mystery of Christ, for which I am also in chains, that I may make it manifest, as I ought to speak. Walk in wisdom toward those who are outside, redeeming the time. Let your speech always be with grace, seasoned with salt, that you may know how you ought to answer each one."

It's like he was thinking about how he should behave while in prison and teaching through his letters at the same time. Paul admonished them to pray that God would open doors for him to preach the gospel. Not open the prison doors. He could have asked for prayer to get out, but he didn't. In other words, he did not harp on the fact that he was in prison, he was about His Father's business no matter where he found himself or what he found himself in at the time. Paul wanted God's word to be made manifest through his experience in prison. Paul was acutely aware of his surroundings. He was surrounded by prisoners who were unbelievers. He had to use wisdom and lay aside his feelings and focus on the task God had given him. He needed to let the prisoners see God at work in him, while he was in prison. He knew they were watching him and that he was not at liberty to do and say anything that would be contrary to what he had been preaching outside of those prison walls. I must say again here that Paul wrote at least one-third of the New Testament, most of which he was suffering whether he was beaten, shipwrecked, persecuted, or imprisoned, he stayed on course.

Paul disciplined himself. He had to be determined not to focus on the chains, but on the people God had assigned and designed for his life to reach. 1 Cor. 4:27 says:

"But I discipline my body and bring it into subjection, lest, when I have preached to others, I myself should become disqualified."

46

We must be disciplined not to complain. We must be disciplined to speak life through all circumstances. We must be disciplined to see in the spirit and walk thereby. We must endure persecution. 2 Timothy 3:10-12 says:

> *"But you have fully known my doctrine, manner of life, purpose, faith, longsuffering, charity, patience, persecutions, afflictions, which came unto me at Antioch, at Iconium, at Lystra; what persecutions I endured: but out of them all the Lord delivered me. Yea, and all that will live godly in Christ Jesus shall suffer persecution."*

You must be convinced that God has a greater purpose "for" us than what man can do "to" us. There are things inside of us that are in a reserve bank, waiting for true manifestation the way Paul explained in Colossians 4. There are things that God will not reveal to you until God needs them. Paul understood that concept. Paul found himself many times in situations that could have rendered complaining, but he had a made up mind to decrease, that it was no longer him that lived, but Christ that lived through him. Paul used what he went through to glorify God, by writing about his experiences as an opportunity to teach us things God enlightened and illuminated to him during those times of hardship. There was no time for the "woe is me, syndrome" Paul's experiences are still helping us today. God purposed him to help many people beyond where he found himself at the time. Perhaps you have found yourself in difficulties that were not your fault, please be careful to allow the Holy Spirit to grace you through it all. Not just to get you through it, but so that as others see it happen to you and witness your behavior it can be used also to help others in difficult times.

What is it that you should be learning in your difficult times in life whether it is or it's not your fault? We must learn and teach through our lives. Paul was just a regular person such as we are. Romans 12:1 says:

"I beseech you therefore, brethren, by the mercies of God,
that you present your bodies a living sacrifice, holy,
acceptable unto God, which is your reasonable service."

A sacrifice gets cuts and bruises. We as living sacrifices will get cut up, torn, chopped, and gutted. As sacrifices get used, but through the process we must die to ourselves and in the end, glorify God. I will even go on to say that "through" it all, we must glorify God. We will be tried and tested as well.

I decided to pass every test and in doing that I knew I needed God to help me and He will not dwell where there is no submission. Therefore, I have to stay submissive, humble, and pliable to His will. Staying in that mindset keeps me aware of the way God wants me to behave and makes a clear distinction between my way and His way, which does not always line up together. Our desire should be to please Him in all our ways. We may have some failures, but we will desire to have another chance to make it right. Many times I have to pray, "Lord give me another chance and help me get it right the next time." He inevitably does. That's what I love about Him, God gives us another and another and another chance. Just humble yourself and receive His counsel and do what He says you should do. What a peace of mind you will begin to have. He knows you better than you know yourself. Forget about what you did before and look forward to what you can do now.

In my exploration of what it takes to keep His will in the forefront of my life and keep Him in the center of my life, I came to the realization that I needed some work. Okay, I must admit, I needed a lot of work. I had to sit down and analyze my life. That took me literally looking at things I did with a different perspective. I had to try to make sure my motives in all I did were pure. You see God really changed me. I want to always please Him in all I do. I was not always that way. I wanted my way and I didn't see any other way. The Holy Spirit comes in and convicts and leads use in the correct way. That's what we need to do at all times. We need to really stop and allow the Holy Spirit to lead us. Life has so many challenges that are overwhelming to us, but the Holy Spirit is never overwhelmed. God can handle whatever we go through.

When you listen to the Holy Spirit, then you begin to walk in the Spirit and not obey the lusts of the flesh. We don't want to be overcome by the challenges of life, but we want to be relentlessly determined to overcome life's challenges.

There was a time in my life that I really didn't know the difference in pleasing God or pleasing man. I was so in touch with the way other people felt, trying to fit in and be accepted that I was not concerned with what God was saying to me. There was a need within me that only God could fulfill, but I foolishly thought by pleasing man, I would be fulfilled and happy.

> *"For do I now persuade men, or God? Or do*
> *I seek to please men? For if I yet pleased men,*
> *I should not be the servant of Christ"*
> Galatians 1:10

I hadn't really allowed Him into every area of my life yet. I was afraid to. I thought of everything I had to give up, ignorantly believing that I was giving up more than I would be gaining. I have since found out the benefits of giving God my whole heart and allowing Him into every area of my life to mold and shape me no matter what man thinks, is the absolute best thing that has ever happened to me. Perhaps that's where you are right now. Perhaps you need to see that there is a distinct difference between His ways and our ways. You have one way of thinking, but God wants to show you His way. I believe it's time for you to make some powerful changes in your life.

These are changes that God will help you to accomplish. Do you think you are spiritually healthy? I know I wasn't at one point in my life and I took drastic changes to make sure I became spiritually healthy. I continue to take drastic steps to maintain my spiritual health. You have to exercise your spiritual muscles in order to be spiritually healthy. Sincerely begin to take a close look at yourself and be honest enough to come to terms with where you really are spiritually.

"He leads the humble in what is right, and
the humble He teaches His way"
Psalm 25:9

As you stay humble, God can get in and make the necessary changes needed for you to be spiritually healthy. It takes you feeding and building on your spirit man continually. You have to be willing to put forth an honest effort to work on yourself and not look at everyone around you. I'm a firm believer of humbling myself under the hand of God so He can show me my flaws and I can get it right through Him and give Him the glory. I certainly never want to be caught with a proud look, a boastful attitude, or an arrogant spirit. 1 Peter 5:5b clearly states:

"Clothe (apron) yourselves, all of you, with humility
[as the garb of a servant, so that its covering cannot
possibly be stripped from you, with freedom from
pride and arrogance] toward one another."

For God sets Himself against the proud (the insolent, the overbearing, the disdainful, the presumptuous, the boastful)-[and He opposes, frustrates, and defeats them], but gives grace (favor, blessing) to the humble." Humility is the way to go after reading and understanding that scripture. I use to get very angry at times and when I did, I did not show humility. I became prideful and would not yield to anyone. That type of anger had to go. I had to choose to allow God to get it out of me and show me His humility. We must use humility to help us to stay balanced and spiritually healthy. It is vitally important to stay balanced. Imbalance is an open door for Satan, who tries to sneak in any way he can.

God showed me my heart a long time ago and the way He revealed it to me opened my eyes vividly to what was in it. This is how God revealed it to me. I saw some sand that was really smooth. It felt pure and clean and warm and flowed with the gentle whisper of the wind. Then I saw this slimy, muddy, sticky dark brown substance that was detestable. I quickly tried to look back at the smooth warm sand, but God wouldn't let me. He said, "Compare the two. Which one would you prefer to have in your heart"? And every time I got angry, that's what He would show me. Just thinking of that quickly made me change my thinking towards what to do with that anger. Anger can be a good thing if you use it against the enemy and not others. Use it to be determined do the will of God. Use it as fuel to burn and to let God's will be done in your life. After all, it's the enemy we are fighting, not each other. So the love walk is a much needed topic that I will be discussing further.

You may say, "What about love, I love people." Yes, but you may love who you want to love, but what about who you don't want to love. Those people who are difficult to love because they simply do not like you, neither do they want to love you back. What about loving those ones that hate you? What about loving those that speak against you? What about loving those that have used and abused you? Can you love the ones that have broken your heart? These are hard probing questions that I have found myself faced with from many times, but God always shows up right on time to line up my thinking to His thinking and my ways to His ways. We must be relentless and determined to let God's will be done through us. God will provide grace and strength to do it. This is when we have to understand that we are to love with God's love because God's love is perfectly flawless. We have to keep that in mind as life hits and hurts. The good news is that it is healthy to love. It's so unhealthy to hate. It's such a waste of valuable time and energy. We need to get busy loving and not hating. We are not going to be effective in the kingdom of God if we don't love God's way. I made up my mind to do just that. Although I have to say that I know it takes more than a made up mind. It literally takes God to come in and do it. It's hard to love when you really don't want to, but through experience, I know when God steps in, He leads you through the process and His grace is sufficient, in that it will enable you to accomplish His will to love, no matter what. I have to use the scripture I used above.

"And God is able to make all grace abound toward you; that you, always having all sufficiency in all things, may abound in every good work"
2 Corinthians 9:8

He will grace you to do the good work He requires of you, to love no matter what. You know, that truth has helped me tremendously. I cannot explain the amount of times I'm faced with people who are difficult to love, but when I call on God's grace, God allows me to do it and it's not hard then because it' s God, not me. God's grace abounds for me to love, love, love and I love it because it feels so good to love. It feels better to love than it does to hate, don't you think? I feel so free now that I have accepted and submitted to God's way to love. Actually many people just need a fresh dose of love to let them know that they do matter and are special. Loving others does so much for the one loving, as well. Your heart is happy and light. Your light is shining. Your spirit is blessed and not grieved. Your life is elevated. You receive the blessings of love.

CHAPTER 3

MAKE IT WORK

"For our light, affliction, which is but for a moment,
is working for us a far more exceeding and eternal
weight of glory, while we do not look at the things which
are seen. For the things which are seen are temporary,
but the things which are not seen are eternal"
Philippians 4:17-18

It is so easy to get entangled with the cares of this world when things get hard and heavy, but God teaches us that He will even make our afflictions work for us. As we trust Him with them, He will take them and help us to gain from them. I am not at all blown away by the afflictions knowing this and meditating on this as much as I used to be. We have to stay steady. To stay steady means trusting God and not trying to handle things right away on our own. We should begin to stand on the truth of God's word no matter what hits us and how hard. It is definitely easy to say when you are not going through a valley experience, but when life happens and things are looking bleak, it gets difficult to remain steady in a mode of trusting in God and His ways. Although I must say that remaining steady and not rushing the process may have you to be in the valley longer than you would like to be, but I always say the valley can be a place that we can gain some great things. In the valley we can get our blessed assurance. In the valley we get our healing, our deliverance, our humility, our patience, our courage, our power to overcome, our faith is strengthened, and our love for God deepens, we gain some tenacity and passion to push. I realized how much He loves me in the valley. So believe God in or out of the valley and know that it is working out for you.

Also, receive everything God has for you in or out of the valley. Of course, no one wants to be in the valley, but now you can look around while you are there and let God bless you through it. You gain the things that are eternal not temporal. So much strength and knowledge is gained as you walk through and learn from every mistake. Try to not be pitiful, but powerful through the whole valley experience because we are powerful in Christ. Just inhale and exhale, keep breathing, it will be okay. Continue to discipline yourself to stay focused on God. The sun will come out tomorrow as the song says. Take some deep breaths and keep it moving through the good and the bad and through all the tough terrain that you have to travel. I'm reminded of so many times when it has gotten hard that the enemy wanted me to stop and hold out on God, but the Holy Spirit would not let me do it. The Holy Spirit held me steady and stable. God will always be there with you. Do not feel alone in any situation. It will work for you if you let it.

"Now thanks be to God who always leads us in triumph in Christ, and through us diffuses the fragrance of His knowledge in every place"
2 Corinthians 2:14

We can rest assured in Him that He will work on our behalf and make it work for our behalf in every place we find ourselves throughout life.

I absolutely love helping people and seeing them experience breakthroughs in their lives. It is one of those things that God uses to keep me going and encouraged that He is working through me using that treasure that He has planted in me for His kingdom. I am encouraged when I see you encouraged. It does my heart good to bless people and allow God to use me in their lives. It truly humbles me because I know I cannot do what He has called me to do without Him. I know that is what God has purposed me to do, which is to be a true blessing in the lives of others, no strings attached because I know where my help comes from. I also believe He blesses me because of that. I am excited about that. When we can put our own interests aside and give a hand to someone else that's truly trusting God. That is the remarkable work of God using us as an extension of His love. Isn't that just the most fulfilling thing we could ever do in life? We can really begin to see God at work in our lives as we begin to let Him be seen through us in the lives of others. He always gives us rewards, but that is a small benefit to being used to really change someone's life for the better and introduce them to the love of Christ. It's not for the reward that we help people, although there are great rewards, but it is because God is in us.

> *"[Not in your own strength] for it is God Who is all the*
> *while effectually at work in you [energizing and creating*
> *in you the power and desire], both to will and to work*
> *for His good pleasure and satisfaction and delight"*
> Philippians 2:13

I'm excited just thinking about it. I am blessed to be a Pastor's wife and I thought going in that it would be a lot to heartache, but to the contrary, I see so many lives get better. I get to participate with God as God transforms lives, marriages, and families through the most difficult of situations. I love how God fixes us up and then uses us to fix others up. As we get fixed up, you know what I mean, during the process we can be used by God to lavish His love on others.

> *"Blessed be God, even the Father of our Lord Jesus*
> *Christ, the Father of mercies, and the God of all comfort;*
> *who comforts us in all our tribulation, that we may be*
> *able to comfort them which are in any trouble, by the*
> *comfort wherewith we ourselves are comforted of God"*
> 2 Corinthians 1:4

Will you be that blessing for someone else as they go through a tough time in their life even though you are going through something? We can use the very same tactics God used on us to help someone else get through their difficulty. That's what it's all about, being that help for others that God has called us to be. You see, we have to trust God and move out on purpose. If we want to have His purpose fulfilled in our lives, then we need to be willing to sacrifice ourselves and let Him deal with our issues as He uses us to help someone else with theirs.

At this very moment, I am going through betrayal, which is so very hurtful, but God told me today to call and encourage three people even though I needed encouragement and as I obeyed His voice, believe it or not, I began to get the encouragement I needed. I feel awesome now. Did the situation change? No, I changed from feeling down and out to being a blessing in someone else's life. Through that God revealed to me that it helps us to help others. We have been programmed by our Maker to have that inside of us so that we can have enthusiasm to help others. He wants us out there in the trenches helping and healing and loving and moving and shaking. Not somewhere closed up, discouraged, let down, and feeling sorry for ourselves. You may think you don't have anything to offer, but God has created you with great purpose and potential. You can help others with what is in your hands to do. Do what you know you can do and God will handle the rest. Just do it. Nike says, "Just do it", but I say, "Let's do it." It will bless you. The gift of encouragement is absolutely powerful. It's not just flattering words or empty praise without substance, but it is heartfelt words that inspire us with hopeful confidence meant to build us up as needed and to enhance our relationship with God and with others. Be an encourager to others. Decide to be that someone in the lives of others that will encourage them and inspire them to go forward no matter what happens.

Someone may have lied to you and told you that you will never amount to anything and you are useless. Don't believe the lie from the enemy. You have a lot to offer. Just go to God and ask Him what is it that He has so graciously He given you to do. He will certainly be obliged to let you know as you search for it. Little by little, and piece by piece, God will begin to show you the real you. You will find yourself doing what comes natural. When you do things for others it's like giving yourself a boost, it makes you feel great and truly fulfilled. We are blessed to be a blessing. Yes, we are blessed when we bless others, but also it is a blessing to be a blessing in someone else's life. I have learned so much about being a blessing to others. God has shown me that being a blessing to someone else is why we were equipped with gifts and talents. Yes, we were created to glorify God, but ultimately glorifying God is helping mankind. That's what God really wants out of us. The enemy hates it when we discover that and decide to do it. The devil wants nothing more than to sabotage us before we actually begin to help others live in victory. You see, our victory means his shame and defeat. God is adamant about making sure we are blessed when we surrender to Him so that we can put the devil to shame and take back what he stole from us and share it with others. The enemy wants us to hate ourselves and defeat ourselves because he knows he cannot. He has no power over us. We need to send him packing every time he shows up. Don't just talk about what he is doing. Defeat him, rebuke him, take authority over him, and leave him hopeless, helpless, and fruitless.

Because of rejection issues, I remember periods of self-loathing. I would spiral down to a depressed state at times in my life and I didn't even like to hear my name being called. I didn't even want to look in the mirror. The enemy told me in first person that I hated myself and I repeated what he told me out loud which brought life to it. I was so down on myself that I was looking for ways to take my life. I never had peace and I wanted to end it. The only thing that kept me alive many times was the fact I had two kids to take care of and I didn't know of anyone else who could care for them the way I would. There were times when my husband had to take sharp objects from me as I held them to my wrist to commit suicide. He literally hid knives from me. Because I didn't love myself, I couldn't properly love anyone. I tried to love, but it was always the wrong way. I was completely dissatisfied with myself and was spiritually empty and weak. I tried to be what people wanted me to be so I would not experience the rejection, but I was not happy at all. Even though I was physically fit and healthy, I needed something else. I needed to get spiritually fit and healthy. I longed for my inside to reflect on the outside. I really and earnestly desired God to heal every area of my life because I knew He could. Why would we stop at a little and settle when we can have it all. Why not allow God to do what it takes to get us spiritually healthy so that we can really begin to explore all God has for us and allow our true destiny to be fulfilled. As we walk in destiny we will continue to strive to be spiritually healthy by always going to the Father for nourishment.

Spiritual health means exercising all the good stuff (gifts) God has given you by using what you have on others to not only help them, but also to strengthen your good stuff (gifts) in the process. You see, the more I help others, and sometimes make mistakes while I'm helping them, I learn how to do it better the next time as I learn from every mistake. I refuse to sit around and live afraid to help people because I'm not perfect. That defeats our God given purpose. We were created to be vessels to help others. He juiced us up with some abilities that no one else can do like us. We have our own way of putting that special touch on something that only we can do. You will receive a blessing, maybe even a deep desire of your heart in return.

We should strive to give in order to be givers. When we give, we are planting a harvest that will grow. The more you give, the more you have to give.

"Give and it will come back to you, good measure,
pressed down shaken together and running over, shall
men give unto your bosom. For with the same measure
that you meet, with it shall be measured to you again"
Luke 6:38

So give and keep on giving. Your motives are pure when you just live to give of yourself for the glory of God. You will begin to love to give, not just things, but of yourself to empower and help others. I think that makes God smile. I think you can really start to see Him move mightily through you for others that way. Go ahead put your hands to the plow and do something special for someone. Out of the goodness of your heart, just do it.

"For a good tree does not bring forth corrupt fruit;
neither does a corrupt tree bring forth good fruit"
Luke 6:43

You have good fruit to bear from your own loins. You have something special in you that God wants to use to make someone else feel special. Don't sit on it. Bless it and give it back to God for His intended use. When you put it in God's hands, He knows how to work it through you and it will definitely bless you.

> *"You are the light of the world. A city that is set on*
> *a hill cannot be hid. Neither do men light a candle,*
> *and put it under a bushel, but on a candlestick;*
> *and it gives light unto all that are in the house"*
> Matthew 5:14-15

Let's talk about the "it" factor. We sometimes look at others and think, wow they have "it", not realizing that we have "it" too. Your treasure is the "it" God put in you. Our "it" may not be the same as theirs, but you better believe you have an "it". You just have to locate it, exercise "it" and work "it." It's that special something you do that you love to do and you do it well with zeal and enthusiasm. When you see others using their "it" to glorify God, begin to analyze yourself by looking on the inside to locate your "it." God will aid you in the process. You too have gifts, talents and special abilities. Think about it, what is it that you enjoy doing that you can use to help others. You got "it" too, use "it." God is not unfair to have a select few that He gives special things for them to do on earth and not to others.

> *"Then Peter opened his mouth, and said, of a truth*
> *I perceive that God is no respecter of persons"*
> Acts 10:34

It's ok to actually love working your "it" too. Like I explained earlier, I love helping others and encouraging them in whatever they may be involved with doing because somehow I know that God is glorified and the Holy Spirit within me is urging me to do it. The Holy Spirit will do what He was sent to do, which is to guide you. Loving it is all a part of the package. You can thrive off of helping others in so many ways. God wants to get the glory so as you begin to trust Him and step out. Don't forget to give Him the glory. Don't forget to recognize your Source. I know you can't wait to explore your "it". Give Him all glory, honor and praise. Please do not allow people to stifle your "it" and make you hold back on God.

Persecution will come, but don't feel like you are the lone ranger or be moved by it. The apostle Paul explains that persecution is to be expected. Persecution is, for the ministers of God, marks of a truly effective ministry. Persecution is a sign that you are truly tapping in and doing the work God has put you here to do and you are a threat to the kingdom of darkness. 2 Corinthians 6:4-10 vividly explains:

> *"But in all things we commend ourselves in every way as true servants of God: through great endurance, in tribulation and suffering, in hardships and privation, in sore straits and calamities, in beatings, imprisonments, riots, labors, sleepless watching, hunger; by innocence and purity, knowledge and spiritual insight, longsuffering and patience, kindness, in the Holy Spirit, in unfeigned love; by speaking the word of truth, in the power of God, with the weapons of righteousness for the right hand [to defend]; Amid honor and dishonor; in defaming and evil report and in praise and good report. [We are branded] as deceivers (imposters), and [yet vindicated as] truthful and honest. [We are treated] as unknown and ignored [by the world], and [yet we are] well-known and recognized [by God and His people]; as dying, and yet here we are alive; as chastened by suffering and [yet] not killed; As grieved and mourning, yet [we are] always rejoicing; as poor [ourselves, yet] bestowing riches on many; as having nothing and [yet in reality] possessing all things."*

Although there is so much persecution explained in that passage, please do not ignore the "yets" that are there. Even though there are persecutions, the "yets" in that passage explain just how ineffective they are in our lives if we stay focused on God and be determined to press on no matter what. Those "yets" speak volumes about the power of God over every tactic of the enemy. None of it will be effective if we continue on in His will. Do not let that stop you or make you abort what God has told you to do. Do not abort. Do not second-guess yourself because it is so easy to change your mind when you do that. Stay plugged in to God and keep your spiritual ear to His mouth. When your treasure has been unveiled and used by God you will encounter some strange things because of it, but just be aware of it and take it all in stride so that God can use it all for your good. You will gain so much strength and experience that will be used to help others in the kingdom who are carrying out their assignments as well. Get your assignment from God Himself and move out in His timing. If you fail, get up and wipe yourself off. Get new orders from God and keep going forward. Focus on God's plan, obtain His grace, and trust Him with your whole heart, knowing that He is there for you. Put a song in your heart and a confession on your lips so that you can keep yourself encouraged. Shine with the brilliance of the One who sent you. Do not let fear grip and stifle you. Grip it, instead and choke the life out of it. You choke it by going ahead on and doing what God put in your heart to do. Fear has stopped me before, but I had to face it to overcome it and now I know that God was with me. Fear has gripped the most valiant and strongest of people. Think of David, the captain of the great armies of Israel, one of the mightiest men of valor. God said of David:

"And when He had deposed him, He raised up David to be their king; of him He bore witness and said, I have found David, son of Jesse, a man after My own heart, who will do all My will and carry out My program fully"
Acts 13:22

Can God say that of you today? Will you step up and be counted as one of God's valiant. I pondered on this scripture and it blew me away that God said, "He found David." What God meant was that through many tests, He concluded the heart of David. God had watched how David tended the sheep. God watched as he slew the Giant and did other great exploits. He did the will of the Father, but not without making mistakes. David had to learn from his mistakes and not allow fear to stop him. Just as David did before trying to fight any army, he asked God if he should pursue. If God said no, he did not proceed. If God said yes, he knew that was like money in the bank and that he was destined to win the battle. He knew he had Almighty God on his side if he got the go ahead to fight. Many times David was out numbered, but God gave him divine strategy on how to pursue and win. Believe it or not, I prayed that prayer over myself many times that God would say of me what He said of David, "I have found Bonita, a woman after my own heart, who will do all My will and carry out my program fully." Isn't that what obedience is all about? Isn't that what God's grace is there for as well? To enable us to do those things that God asks of us that we feel we are incapable of doing? God's grace is our empowered ability to do the impossible. Our empowerment comes from the grace of God. I call on grace every time I can't do it. God wants us to understand that through His dynamic grace, we are empowered to do everything He tells us to do. I love it. I simply cannot get enough of hearing and seeing God move in the lives of His people. It's astonishing to see and hear what God does. I'm a believer. I'm completely convinced. You can be too. You can experience God move for you in the most profound ways. Just trust Him. He won't let you down. The only way to know is to take that step of faith and keep on stepping. It will be difficult at times, but never give up. Luke 9:62 says:

> "Jesus said to him, No one who puts his hand to the plow and looks back [to things behind] is fit for the kingdom."

At this very moment, I'm thanking God for reminding me of that scripture so I can continue to keep moving forward. Take it one day and one situation at a time. Ask for God's perspective on everything because our perspective can be a little shaded according on what we have been through. When God gives you His thoughts and ways, believe what He shows you and speak what He says and step, step, step. There will be times when you will have to step slower than you would like, but the thing to do is step and let God dictate your pace. The process will then begin to make sense and come together just as God planned. There is so much I really do not understand right now in my life, but I believe God. I will not be hindered by not knowing. We must trust and believe that He is everything we need. When the enemy tries to make you doubt what you are doing and make you feel like the problem he put in your way is insurmountable, just tell him "I AM" sent you. God is everything you need to overcome every obstacle the devil tries to put in your path to hinder you. Take authority over him. Apply the blood over the problem and yourself. Dig deep within and watch God show up for you. You will experience God in a whole new way every time. It is simply amazing what God will do for you as you begin to step out on faith to believe and do His will.

Fear will make you think you have to do everything perfectly.

> *"There is no fear in love, but perfect love casts out fear. For fear has to do with punishment, and whoever fears has not been perfected in love"*
> 1 John 4:18

God's love for you will help you to overcome all sorts of fears. Believe me I know because I had all sorts of fears that only the love of God removed from me. My struggle with fear almost ruined my life, as I was so afraid of failure that it stifled my growth at one point. Why did it stifle my growth? Well, I used to have to see it to believe it. I could not get past the natural, which in turn stopped me from ever stepping out on faith and believing God for something supernatural. I had to seek God about that debilitating fear that takes the life and livelihood out of you. It impedes adventure and spontaneity. There are so many different kinds of fears out there. Fear of the dark, fear of heights, fear of confined places, fear of public places, fear of failure, fear of sickness, fear of being wrong, fear of not knowing (the unknown). Some of these may seem unreal to you, but they are agonizingly real to masses of people. As close as David was to God, no matter how intimate, He still had fears. He just did not tolerate them. David refused to allow them to overtake him to the point of quitting. It took him continually seeking God for strength and guidance, every step of the way and I submit to you that we have to do the same in order to complete our assignments. Make it a habit to get in His presence just to gain whatever you may need at the time. Sometimes it's difficult to really put your finger on what you really need, but believe me God is well aware of what we need and He will supply it according to His riches in glory. God is rich in whatever we need.

> *"I sought the Lord, and He heard me,*
> *and delivered me from all my fears"*
> Psalms 34:4

David accomplished great exploits for God as captain of the army of Israel. He had defeated armies upon armies of men, yet he still had fears that God had to deliver him from. Face fear head on and defeat it. Do not tolerate it or it will stifle you. I'm reminded of a sermon I once heard where the pastor exclaimed over and over again, emphatically, "Fear tolerated is faith contaminated!" You must do the opposite of what fear wants you to do in order to fight it. Fight fear with faith and boldness. By that I mean faith steps, big or small steps. Timing and season is important. Do not let the enemy hold you back or slow you down. Trust God and pull on His power to move forward. The power of God will catapult you, kick you, push you, and pull you forward. Fear is a struggle that many of us have to face, but by the grace of God we can wiggle loose and break free from it. We must live completely free of the stifling fear the enemy uses to stop us.

CHAPTER 4

WHATEVER THE COST

*"For it is God who works in you both to
will and to do for His good pleasure"*
Philippians 2:13

Please understand it is God working in you to do what He wants
you to do and it will be Him to bring it to pass. I know you have heard
that so many times before, but you have to believe that it's true and
continue to stay focused on God and what He is saying in order that
you may obey His voice in what He has called you to do. What God is
saying to you won't be easy, and it may seem impossible, but with God,
it is possible.

*"But Jesus looked at them and said,
"With men it is impossible, but not with God;
for with God all things are possible"*
Mark 10:27

The opinion of man is not the mind of God. Get the mind and heart
of God and run with it. When it starts to prosper, you will find that evil
will surface out of people. "Blessed are they which are persecuted for
righteousness' sake: for theirs is the kingdom of heaven. Stay kingdom
minded and do kingdom work. The kingdom awaits you. Get up and
get going. I must emphasize here again as I explained earlier, do not
second guess yourself because that is what's stopping so many people
from going forward or even being on time for a move of God. Second

guessing myself has stopped me on numerous occasions. It continually tries to stop me, but to no avail. I continue to strive, press, and push forward. You must do the same. Listen, if we don't get pass what we need to get pass, we won't move forward in the things we need to move forward with. It's as simple as that. All the "what if's" will have to take a back seat to the power of God and put the Holy Spirit in the driver's seat to steer you into all truth so you can experience your destiny.

You may think, well I don't have any support or anyone to encourage me. I thought that many times, but God usually doesn't announce to everyone what He is instructing you to do. You may even sound crazy to yourself when you say what God wants you to accomplish through Him, but keep on pressing. It will come to pass. When you get discouraged, stand up and begin to encourage yourself in the Lord.

> *"Why am I discouraged? Why is my heart so*
> *sad? I will put my hope in God! I will praise*
> *him again—my Savior and my God!"*
> Psalm 43:5

God is your hope, not man. Sure there will be times when man will come by to encouraged you, but don't rely on that to happen every time you need to be encouraged. By the way, when they did come to encourage you, it was God who sent them. God will take you through scripture to encourage you. You then should speak those scriptures out loud so faith can come over and over again as you hear the spoken word. Every time you feel like giving up. You need to be sure of who God is in your life and place your hope in Him. Hope in God is the reassurance you need to keep on moving when you feel like stopping. Don't give up because God is watching and waiting on you to call Him to your rescue. Then God will give you the rest of the story. Little by little, step-by-step you will reach your goal. I remember one day waking up one morning after receiving some bad news the day before and I felt so discouraged and let down. I was being persecuted and betrayed by the very people that I helped the most and loved dearly. I began to press in to God's presence, I prayed and God gave me the same instruction that I wrote about earlier, which was to call three people and encourage them and then get off the phone. The three, He said represented the Father, the Son and the Holy Spirit. He also said to immediately get off the phone after I encourage them so that I would not talk about the incident, which He advised me would not help the situation. I obeyed and immediately after the last call, I felt a burst of energy that was so invigorating and captivating that I began to write more and hear from Him clearly. I gained so much from that time of persecution that I could ever have imagined. It gave me more strength to endure through various trials. It gave me more power to press forward during adversity. It showed me that God is for me and no one can be against me. It helped me to understand how important my treasure was to the kingdom of God. I have to admit, I never thought God would use such hurt and pain to allow me to gain so much. You should be reminded that during adversity God should be your main source of support. Please understand that those are the times that you gain the most from God to endure hardships. When you are persecuted for righteousness sake, you sometimes cannot see that the reason why you are going through is because you are making a difference and the enemy hates it. Suffering is one of the most difficult things to understand when you are going through it. You can very easily get caught up in a pity party and think, woe is me. I just get treated so badly. I am so alone in this. No one understands what I'm going through. No one cares about me. I can recall thinking those things, but then God comes in after I begin to meditate on Him and teaches me such great lessons and helps me to see things on a grander scale from His perspective. He had to change my attitude concerning suffering. God is not pleased by us suffering, but we honor Him and He is pleased when we endure with a better attitude than having a "woe is me" mentality. My perspective of the "woe is me" mentality, would not have given God any glory, but when I thought of God getting the glory, I began to see myself as being a living sacrifice for Him. 1 Peter 2:19-20 says:

> *"For one is regarded favorably (is approved, acceptable,
> and thankworthy) if, as in the sight of God, he endures
> the pain of unjust suffering. [After all] what kind of glory*

[is there in it] if, when you do wrong and are punished
for it, you take it patiently? But if you bear patiently
with suffering [which results] when you do right and that
is undeserved, it is acceptable and pleasing to God."

Please be reminded of your overall goal when you are suffering and keep a clear perspective as you seek God for guidance and counseling about what you are going through. There are going to be many occasions to think wrong about what you go through, but stick to the plan of God for your life.

Distractions are going to come in order to get you off course, but you cannot let them do what they came to do. People will be put in your life to distract and discourage you. Put them away from you and press with all diligence. There has got to be something on the inside of you to drive you. You cannot always depend on other people to move you or encourage you. Sure, God will use others, but He doesn't want them to be your driving force because He knows how fickle people can be and He also knows they can't be what He can be for you. Let God drive you forward by leaning and depending totally on Him. Let God be that sole source of support that will send you resources to help you. He is everywhere all the time and will push when you need a push. He will kick you when you need a kick and comfort when comfort is needed. Sometimes people will comfort when you need a kick and kick when you need comfort. God sees and knows what you are going through. He is acutely aware of the people around you. He is very concerned about your suffering and is ready to come to your defense. 1 Peter 3:12 explains:

"For the eyes of the Lord are over the righteous,
and His ears are open to their prayers: but the face
of the Lord is against them that do evil."

People are not getting away with persecuting you or distracting you. God has a way of dealing with them as only He can do. Leave them to God. He's got you. Do not take God's vengeance, but let God take vengeance. He will repay. Stay focused on your goal. There is no need for you to get off course or get them back. Evil begets evil and that does not glorify God at all. It's very clear to me now that when I am getting ready to do something major for God, I get persecuted and the enemy tries to distract me. It is a major distraction to get off track of the will of God to do evil against the person or people the enemy uses to bring you down. When someone is doing evil against you, pray and forgive, but most importantly, keep going forward. Do not allow the distractions to deter your attention away from the will of God. Try your very best to not look to the left or the right so that you will stay the course. 1 Peter 3:9 states:

"Not rendering evil for evil, or railing for railing:
but contrariwise blessing, knowing that you are
thereunto called, that you should inherit a blessing."

So let them keep doing evil, while you keep inheriting a sweet blessing. What a great exchange. Glory to God.

My inspiration comes when I am in the worst of times it seems. I seem to want to push even harder and strive even harder. It's not me in me, it's Jesus in me. Jesus is a force to be reckoned with. Jesus is that driving force that no foe can withstand. Jesus will give you confidence, character, and charisma. Whatever it takes, He's got it. Whatever you need, He's got it. Just call Him because sometimes we don't even know what we need, but He does.

"Call to Me and I will answer you and
show you great and mighty things, fenced in and
hidden, which you do not know (do not distinguish
and recognize, have knowledge of and understand)"
Jeremiah 33:3

I don't know about you, but I think I'm going to do just that. I continue to call on Him and ask for help. It never fails, He always comes to my rescue. You have to realize what a blessing it is to rely on the power of God. Presently, when God shows me something that needs to be done, I rely on Him to show me how and when. I say presently because it has not always been that way. I have prayed about things and He has shown me what I should do. I'm learning to trust Him fully, no matter the cost because it always ends up being the very thing that moves me forward to the next level. I admonish you to do the same. I urge you to be vigilant in doing exactly what God says and how He says it and see won't the end result be very attractive to you.

If your reservations are from fear, then do this. Do it anyway! Don't allow fear to stifle you. The enemy uses fear the way God uses faith. Faith encourages you to do, but fear discourages you from doing. Be assured that you will be blessed as you do the will of God. James 1:25 says:

> *"But if you look into the perfect law of liberty that sets you free, and if you do what it says and don't forget what you heard, then God will bless you for doing it."*

I don't think it can get any plainer than that. God's perfect law is the fulfillment of the Old Testament. Christ fulfills the "perfect law" because He was the only person who qualified. No matter how difficult it was. Jesus was determined to fulfill it because that was His purpose for being sent here on earth. The same is true for us. When we find purpose, we must pursue it. Those who come to Him by faith therefore have true freedom from the bondage of sin and any bondage that will come to keep you stuck and not obey the leading of the Holy Spirit. Jesus Christ Himself set us free and gave us true liberty. We don't have to follow what man says makes sense. We are free to serve God with our whole heart and that entails doing His will His way and in His timing. I think that freedom also gives us so many other privileges and benefits to steward what God has given us and be diligent to fulfill our purpose as well. What awesome power we have at our disposal. What infinite wonders He wants to perform concerning us. I want to live diligently and purposely helping others. I want to show God that I am not afraid to believe and trust Him even if I don't quite get it right all the time. That's why His unconditional love is so vital. Truly understanding God's unconditional love for me liberated me in so many ways. God's love relaxes me into knowing that I can mess up and He not hold it over my head and turn His back on me. God's love casts away all fear. God's love eliminates the possibility of anyone or any weapon prospering against me. We have to decide not to allow pride to set in and make us not admit to our mistakes so we can ask for forgiveness and move on, knowing that God loves us unconditionally. That is truly enough to keep me moving and pressing forward. Once you truly receive God's love in your spirit, you can overcome fear. First John 4:18 says:

> *"There is no fear in love;*
> *but perfect love casts out fear: because fear has torment.*
> *He that fears is not made perfect in love."*

You must understand that fear has no place in your life. It is foreign to us as believers. God's love expels every trace of it. Glory to the King! That truth creates a flow of obedience in your life that fear cannot stop. Allow your faith to override fear. God has not given us fear. It comes directly from the enemy. 2 Timothy 1:7 says:

> *"For God has not given us a spirit of fear, but of*
> *power and of love and of a sound mind."*

Keep moving forward, pressing, believing, and receiving.

You see, the blessing is in the pressing. When you press against pressure and continue to move forward regardless of the pressure, you gain strength from the pressure as you advance forward. When the pressure gets to be too much, God is ready to immediately step in at the point of your weakness and His strength will be made perfect. Moving forward shows that you not only withstood the pressure, but that you used the strength to push, which results in you becoming stronger because you exerted more strength. So yes, the pressure is definitely, in so many ways, working for you. Glory to God! I think I'm going to stop here and shout, Hallelujah! I think I will dance along with that, hallelujah!

Let's look now at Peter when Herod the king was trying to torment the church by killing the disciples. King Herod had decided to stop

Peter because Peter was being used mightily and the church was growing and more and more believers were added to the body. Acts 12:1, 4 says:

"About that time Herod the king stretched forth his hands to afflict and oppress and torment some who belonged to the church (assembly)."

And when he had seized [Peter], he put him in prison and delivered him to four squads of soldiers of four each to guard him, purposing after the Passover to bring him forth to the people. Herod wanted to make a name for himself and make himself look powerful before the people by slaying Peter in front of them. Little did he know that God had a plan. Little did he know that he was not more powerful than God. God was not concerned with how many guards he had wrapped around Peter. Let's read on to find out God's great plan.

"The very night before Herod was about to bring him forth, Peter was sleeping between two soldiers, fastened with two chains, and sentries before the door were guarding the prison. And suddenly an angel of the Lord appeared [standing beside him], and a light shone in the place where he was. And the angel gently smote Peter on the side and awakened him, saying, Get up quickly! And the chains fell off his hands"
Acts 12:6-7

I like that he "gently" smote Peter. He just tapped him to wake him up. Nothing can withstand the power of God. God is Almighty, and therefore is never limited by how hard it may be to get you out of or to help you through a situation. Nothing can stop God when He is coming to your rescue. He will do what it takes to free you or aid you and allow you to continue on in His will. Man can never hem you in unless you give man the power to do so. Peter trusted God. Of all the guards Peter had around him and the chains that had him bound, Peter remained calm and went to sleep trusting God. Peter was not crying and heaving all night worried and frantic about what he was experiencing. He simply trusted God and went to sleep. Sure he may have been afraid, but he still went to sleep. He conquered the fear instead of allowing the fear to torment and overtake him, making him stay up all night worrying or fretting and wondering how in the world am I going to get out of this. That shows complete trust in God. We should all use this situation to encourage us that as long as God is for us, we are the majority. We are never stuck in any situation where God is concerned. God is waiting to rescue you out of all you find yourself against. God is willing to maneuver and pull you through the toughest of times. It didn't matter how great of number of guards or how closely chained to the soldiers Peter was, God was able to send an angel and His light shined through and gave Peter his freedom from all the bondage Herod thought he had around Peter. What an amazing truth. Please get this. Please reflect on the very things or people that make you feel stuck or bound and call the name of Jesus. Trust God with it all. Quickly be obedient to what God tells you to do, as the angel told Peter to quickly get up because delayed obedience is still disobedience. When Peter quickly got up, the chains immediately fell off. Timing is of the essence when obeying God. Sometimes situations drag on in our lives because we drag our feet when it comes to obeying God. As you obey, your help will show up at the right time needed just like Peters' did. You may not know where or what to do to get the help you need, but God does and will give you everything you need to succeed. Right now, just take the time to stop and give everything you are dealing with to God. At this point, as God is showing you that He is for you. God wants to take what you have and free you from it so you can serve Him free of everything that is trying to hold you down in bondage.

Many times I look back and reflect on some things I've gone through in the past and think, how did I make it through that? Then I begin to reflect on God's hand through it all and just bask in God's glory because I know it would not have been possible without the grace of God. We have to stop mentally living in the past and begin to think in agreement with God. Then once we do that we can then speak in agreement with Him. We can then prophesy our future because we have come into agreement with God. Isaiah 43:19 says:

*"Behold, I am doing a new thing! Now it springs
forth; do you not perceive and know it and will
you not give heed to it? I will even make a way
in the wilderness and rivers in the desert."*

If God can make a way in the wilderness and rivers in the desert, surely
He can make a way for you as you persist to complete His will. A new
thing He can do as we come into agreement with His word. He will use
His scripture to show you How He is going to sculpt your life as you begin
to quote the word with all diligence. Let nothing stop you from quoting
the word of God. You are never boxed in without a way out because He
makes a way when there seems to be no way. If He has to, He will carve
out a way. Maybe you just can't see a way and He has to show you the
way, whatever it takes, there is always a way in Christ. He has done it for
me countless times and I'm so grateful for that. You may be facing what
seems to be a dead end right now, whether financially, emotionally, or
even relationally, but if you will put your trust in God and keep going in
faith, even when you do not see a way, He will be there when you need
Him and God will make a way. Can you imagine Moses and the Israelites
running toward the Red Sea knowing it was there, but had to keep on
going because their life depended on it and Moses knew God had set
His people free. God parted the Red Sea for them and they crossed on
dry ground and when the Egyptians tried to follow, God closed the sea
in on them and well, let's just say, they didn't make it. You may not have
the whole story of how things are going to turn out, but by faith keep it
moving and pray for divine strategy. It will become more understandable
as you keep going down the path He sets before you, but you don't have
to understand to start down the path. Psalms 119:105 says:

"Thy word is a lamp unto my feet and a light unto my path."

It also says in Isaiah 45:2:

*"I will go before you, and make the crooked
places straight: I will break in pieces the gates
of brass, and cut through bars of iron."*

Nothing can withstand God. I say to you, by all means keep pressing and moving with these scriptures in mind. What is your Red Sea? What is the barrier the enemy is trying to use to stop you? Whatever it may be, call Almighty, He will come to your rescue and defeat the enemy on every hand. The power we have at our disposal through Christ is undefeatable. What a glorious resolve. Just ponder on that a minute and see won't you be able to leap over walls and bring down strongholds.

When persecutions come, God has so many promises in His word to help you overcome them. Jesus, His disciples, and the prophets were also resisted by the Pharisees, the Scribes, and the Sadducees, to name a few. They never looked back, but pressed through the pressure. You have to do the same. You have to know that anything worth doing or having in Christ is going to encounter some persecution. You have to know that adversity will come, but do not be moved out of place or intimidated by it. Use it as ammunition to fuel your tank and burst you forward with powerful momentum into that new thing God has for you. The greatest people suffered great persecution, but by the grace of God it didn't stop them. Being persecuted actually makes the blessing even sweeter.

> *"Blessed are you, when men shall hate you, and when they shall separate you from their company, and shall reproach you, and cast out your name as evil, for the Son of man's sake"*
> Luke 6:22

"Blessed" means happy, and it would seem contradictory to find happiness in persecution. Just think, this is actually saying that you are blessed when men are persecuting you. Most Christians are really hesitant to do anything that may make them less popular with others or may lead them to being ostracized and criticized by others, yet it is acceptable to God. Expect to be persecuted, but know what the word says about persecution and that it is inevitable when you are accomplishing kingdom work. Don't shy away from it. Don't make excuses to quit like I used to do. It would be easy to quit when things get hard and dirt is thrown in your face when you are just trying to help people. You will definitely want to just give up and walk away, but something on the inside of you, the Holy Spirit, will kick in and make you get up and get going again. God will make sure of that because He knows it will be needed. God knows we need a jump-start every now and then and He is ready to give it to us through the Holy Spirit. I must reiterate this scripture, 1 Peter 2:20 says:

"For what glory is it if, when you be buffeted for your faults
you shall take it patiently? But if, when you do well, and
suffer for it, you take it patiently, this is acceptable with God."

Although God does not delight in our suffering, God is honored and pleased with your well doing as you go through it with a good attitude. You must trust God through it all. There are times when you will want to know why, but if we had all the answers, faith would not be necessary. Unjust suffering is the worse. Believe me I am truly acquainted with unjust suffering. God sacrificed His Son knowing He would go through unjust and unspeakable suffering, and He did it for us. You may not see the reward now, but later on you will see it work together for your good. The ultimate test of our faith is how we behave during tests, trials and tribulations (The 3-T's), especially when they feel completely unfair. Peter explained to us the fact that fiery trials will come to test the quality of our faith and that we are not to be amazed and bewildered by them. 1 Peter 4:12-13 says:

"Beloved think it not strange concerning the fiery trials which
is to try you, as though some strange thing happened to you:
But rejoice in that you partake of Christ sufferings, that when
His glory is revealed, ye may be glad also with exceeding joy."

Do not be overly concerned about why you are suffering, instead make a determined decision to get through it with a good attitude and you will see God work everything together for your good. You will gain kudos with God even though it seems that you are doing what is right and things are not going well with you because of it. God has a way of rewarding you openly. God has a way of reassuring you that you are on the right track. God has a way of getting things done for you so you can keep going and gain strength. You will have a blessed assurance to jump over walls and leap over hurdles. Even though you may not be pleasing to man sometimes, God is pleased by your good work. Galatians 1:10 says:

"For do I now persuade men, or God?
Or do I seek to please men? For if I pleased men,
I should not be the servant of Christ."

I get excited when I know God is pleased with me. Sometimes you just have to stop and reflect on what is being accomplished so you can gain a better perspective and get invigorated for the cause. Get excited when you know you are doing the will of God, no matter the cost. Get charged up with enthusiasm when you are doing the things God told you to do. Be encouraged when you are persecuted. Use it to be determined to take a licking and keep on ticking. Also think of the Apostles, on one occasion when they were commanded by the Sanhedrin Counsel not to teach in the name of Jesus, Peter and the other apostles responded to them in Acts 5:29-30 this way:

"Then Peter and the other Apostles answered and said,
We ought to obey God rather than men. The God of our
fathers raised up Jesus, whom you slew and hanged on a tree."

They then captured the Apostles, but God raised up one of their own, Gamaliel, a Pharisee and Doctor of the law to defend them. Here's what he said in Acts 5:38-39:

"Now in the present case let me say to you, stand off
(withdraw) from these men and let them alone. For if this
doctrine or purpose or undertaking or movement is of human
origin, it will fail (be overthrown and come to nothing);
But if it is of God, you will not be able to stop or overthrow or
destroy them, you might even be found fighting against God!"

I like the strategy God used here. God used a Doctor of the law to defend them because first of all, God knew they would listen to him and secondly God knew that Gamaliel knew exactly what terminology to use to get to them. He helped them to understand that they could be coming against God himself. The Sanhedrin believed in and feared God, but not Jesus. Now this is the part I am most excited about. They took Gamaliel's advice, but before they let them go this is what transpired, Acts 5:40-42:

> *"And to him they agreed: and when they had called the apostles, and beaten them, they commanded that they should not speak in the name of Jesus, and let them go. And they departed from the presence of the council, rejoicing that they were counted worthy to suffer shame for his name. And daily in the temple, and in every house, they ceased not to teach and preach Jesus Christ."*

They literally got beaten for righteousness sake, but they left the place rejoicing. Isn't that amazing? Can you picture that? The grace of God showed up for them and enabled them to take the beating. The Apostles understood why they were being beaten. They were determined even more to spread the good news of the Gospel of Jesus Christ. They never ceased for a single day to teach of the Gospel of Jesus. You may suffer, but continue on just as the Apostles did. Your job will still be the same when it's all said and done and that is following through with what you started for the Lord with excellence. I remember a time at work when I was a Physical Therapy Technician. I was called into my boss' office due to a complaint that had been filed against me. I prayed before I went in and God gave me peace as I entered the office. My supervisor explained the complaint to me. He told me that someone complained that I was witnessing too much. It was all I could do not to laugh because the story about the Apostles immediately came to my spirit. I listened thoroughly to the complaint, and told my supervisor yes, I am guilty as charged. I told him that I will always witness the Gospel, when given the opportunity. I said that these patients need more than Physical Therapy, they need Spiritual Therapy more. You see my supervisor knew that we had patients that had Post Traumatic Stress Disorder (PTSD). It was an Army hospital and the soldiers were just coming back from Iraq and Afghanistan fighting for our country, but many were diagnosed with this disorder because of what they had experienced over there. I had to pray for many of them and their families. I began to explain to him as they ask me how to deal with their problems while I am caring for them, I proceed to give them biblical answers to their problems. God used me as an intercessor for them. They would call me over to their table to talk and ask for prayer, even if they weren't my patient. God used me mightily in intercession for them on countless occasions. As they began to get breakthroughs, they would always come and share it with me. That's what I know to work because that's what I used and if anyone happens to be listening, I can't do anything about that. He then began to apologize for having to do it and he completely understood my point of view. He also told me that his father was a Pastor and although he didn't act like it, he grew up a Christian. You see God used that to remind him of who he was and to convict him of his lifestyle. I told him it's never too late to start all over and God will forgive him and help him with his problems as well. I left that office smiling from ear to ear because I had been counted worthy to suffer for righteousness sake. That made my day. Instead of being discouraged, which is what the enemy wanted, I rejoiced. That is one day I will never forget. Through Christ, you can follow through to the end that you may see the good come to pass. Your discovered treasure will draw persecution because it is what is most effective in your life for the kingdom. They are even going to talk about you and try to belittle you, but go to God as your refuge. Matthew 10:16 says:

> *"Behold I send you out as sheep in the midst of wolves.*
> *Therefore be wise as serpents and harmless as doves."*

God sends you out as sheep and you may think at times that you are around other sheep, but then you come to realize that they were wolves all along in sheep's clothing. Please don't be surprised if it turns out to be someone close to you doing it or someone you would least expect. God already knows what's going to happen and is waiting to be your present help. The enemy does not discriminate. He will use whoever he can and if it's someone close that will fall prey to his tactics, then even the more effective he thinks he will be, but he is defeated before he gets started. He may have them, but don't let him have you. Forgive and love them anyway. That will help you more than revenge or wasting precious time and energy talking about it and being distracted. You just continue to stay focused on God and on the mission.

Your treasure is so detrimental to the enemy that he will do anything to keep you from it because he knows as you discover your treasure and become proficient in using your treasure, you will see more godly results than you could ever imagine. You will begin to gain souls for the Kingdom of God. I could never have imagined myself praying for someone to be free of the spirit of suicide, but God has used me in prayer to help so many people. First I had to lay hands on myself to not commit suicide because I was suicidal for many years and no one knew it, but my husband and to be honest, I don't think he truly knew how close I came to committing suicide many times, but God always brought my thinking into perspective when He would have me to think of my children and my husband that I would leave behind. I didn't know it wasn't really me that wanted to commit suicide that it was really the enemy relentlessly trying to kill me and use me to do it. When God showed that to me then I asked Him why. Then God showed me a vivid picture of a vision of me in the future ministering and helping many women. Those women would then begin to help other women and on and on. I understood then, why the enemy wanted me to kill myself. I had to press in to Gods presence and let Him pour His love inside of me. God kept telling me to trust Him no matter what I went through. My spirit man needed to find balance and peace. I needed to become spiritually healthy.

Becoming spiritually healthy means balancing it all out so that God will get the glory no matter what it takes. I have resigned to the fact that I want God to get glory out of the good, the bad, and the ugly. Yes, it gets extremely hard and it is sometimes disheartening, but God will bring times of refreshing. Take time to laugh and play. Don't be so serious about everything. My son, Drake said to me one day when I was making a big deal out of a small matter, "It's not that serious, Mom." I thought about it and laughed as I thought, "you know you are absolutely right." That statement really stuck with me. I was able to lighten up when I was getting frustrated about some small matter and not allow the enemy to use it to distract me any longer. Drake is very calm about things so at that moment I appreciated his demeanor and went with it.

God will mend the broken places. He loves loving on us. He takes everything we give Him and orchestrates a perfect plan for survival. We just have to believe that when we truly let go and give God whatever difficult situation it may be that hinders us, He is more than able to handle it. God will do what it takes to make it better for us that He may get the glory.

Think about Jesus as He walked here on earth. He was certainly persecuted. What about all the Apostles and Prophets? The bible is full of stories of the Apostles and Prophets going through persecution. I just want to know why we think it will be any different for us. I used to think, as long as I served God and not bother anyone, no one would bother me. I thought serving God would be a bed of roses. I thought I could just do the will of the Father and all things would just be okay. Well, not so. Contrary to my belief system, it was the exact opposite. If you think the enemy is going to sit idle while you go about saving lives and doing what God has created you to do, then you are in for a rude awakening, as my mom would put it. The very fact that you have decided to love and serve God is a threat to the enemy. The good news is that:

"No weapon that is formed against you will prosper"
Isaiah 54:17a

Once you know that, you can press through and trust God every step of the way. Don't let the enemy overwhelm you with difficulties. It is just a façade, or a smoke screen designed to convince you to give up. Get in the presence of God and defeat him on every hand. You have to find yourself before His face continually in order to overcome. Stay on track with God's plan for your life. Your treasure will be revealed inside of you and give you that extra encouragement that you are chosen and specially equipped to complete your purpose.

> *"Therefore, my beloved brethren, be firm (steadfast), immovable, always abounding in the work of the Lord [always being superior, excelling, doing more than enough in the service of the Lord], knowing and being continually aware that your labor in the Lord is not futile [it is never wasted or to no purpose]"*
> 1 Corinthians 15:58

I like being superior, excelling, and doing more than enough. Don't just do enough to get by. Turn it up for God. Go all out with zeal and passionate conviction. By that I mean with a firm determination to do the will of the Lord. That's the real test. Will you stop short of the will of God in your life because of difficulties or will you press through them. Look in the Spirit, hear what the Lord says and move out accordingly. You will find that most of the difficulties weren't so difficult when the grace of God shows up. His grace is sufficient in everything you go through because it will rise to every occasion to show God's power. 2 Corinthians 12:9 says:

> *"And he said unto me, My grace is sufficient for thee: for my strength is made perfect in weakness."*

I thank God that He even makes provision for our weaknesses. His strength shows up for us when we call Him. There is nothing too hard for God. I love it.

It's a blessing to serve God. It's an honor to be chosen by God to do His work. The Apostles knew this all too well. They were constantly persecuted, and beaten for Christ's sake. They knew it was an honor to be chosen by God. They were not ashamed of the gospel of Christ. They were not intimidated by man, or the tactics of the enemy. They kept moving and trusting in God. That is how God wants us to be as modern day disciples. Ready and willing to do whatever it takes to carry out His will. We must stay ready. We must be very prayerful and I do mean full of prayer. When persecution hurts, and it will, let God come in and comfort you through it all. The enemy will use whomever he can to get to you. Do not be vulnerable to the hurt. Continue to cry out to God and praise Him. Praise God for the victory. Remember, you are not a "victim", but a "victor". There will be plenty of times when you want to give up, but do not let things get to you to the point of destroying or abandoning the plan of God for your life. Don't let the process make you back out on God. Some people give up at the first sign of adversity. Some people let circumstances make them feel like they did not hear from God and they give up because of pressure. Be persistent through the pressure. Prepare to be prepared. What I mean by that is prepare for things to happen to divert or distract you, but be prepared to move past it all and let God show Himself stronger than anything you have to go through to achieve that expected end. Preparing to be prepared also means being ready for those times when you have to ministry unexpectedly. You have to be able to roll with the punches. Preparing is praying before, during, and after your goal is complete. Prayer is a force to be reckoned with. Love also is a power force. Worship Him as you move forward. Listen carefully to instruction and if you mess up, please do not stop. Get back up and keep going until you get it right. Do not underestimate the presence of God. Get alone in His presence often. There is a preplanned, predetermined end to your persecution, but you must persevere.

"When you pass through the waters, I will be with you,
and through the rivers, they will not overwhelm you.
When you walk through the fire, you will not be burned
or scorched, nor will the flame kindle upon you"
Isaiah 43:2

God lets us know that as we go through water and fire, He is with us. There are trials and tests that we will have to go through that are inevitable. It will not be always be a bed of roses. There will be difficult things that we will have to face, but don't forget, you are a winner and God is for you.

Whatever challenges specifically that you will have to face are meant to strengthen you, to develop your character, and to cause you to be able to persevere. They will be used to purify and sanctify you, to teach you some unique lessons of sufferings, to teach discipline and sacrificial benefits, and to make you better. Please understand there are powerful lessons to be learned through the challenges we face. They are meant to make us better not bitter. I have faced many times of betrayal, loneliness, obstacles, and so much persecution. Countless times that I came so close to giving up. There have been people in my life that I just did not care to be around because of the persecution. I am now aware of the fact that those people were near me to burn off some dross and to smooth some of my rough edges. Again I must bring your attention to 1 Peter 4:12-13 that says:

"Beloved, do not be amazed and bewildered at the fiery ordeal which is taking place to test your quality, as though something strange (unusual and alien to you and your position) were befalling you. But insofar as you are sharing Christ's sufferings, rejoice, so that when His glory [full radiance and splendor] is revealed, you may also rejoice with triumph [exultantly]."

I really love that scripture. Glory to God, I can quote it verbatim. Just thought I would give myself some love and pat myself on the back a little. Whatever you go through, you are victorious because of the finished work of the cross, so press, believe, and get the blessing on the other end of your struggle. There is a blessing in being used for the kingdom. This is a blessing that man cannot buy. Pass the test. Burn the dross. Learn the lesson. Earn the T-shirt. Your joy will then be unspeakable and full of glory.

Are you in the middle of something or around someone that God has allowed in your life to use as sandpaper? Remember to look within.

"Search me, O God, and know my heart: try me, and know my thoughts: And see if there be any wicked way in me, and lead me in the way everlasting"
Psalms 139:23-24

Although there may be some wrong on the other person's part, what is it revealing inside of you that need to be worked on by God? You will definitely feel the burn. Believe me, God is going to use it to strengthen you. God is going to use it to change you where you need to be changed. God is going to use it to advance you into His purpose for your life. No one wants to go through difficulties, but they are necessary to get you to destiny. Please be aware God will use these things or people in order that He can take you, break you and then make you. Although God gives gifts to us, good fruit and godly character has to be developed. Character is defined as the way someone thinks, feels, and behaves. Our thinking has to start lining up with the word of God and the way God thinks. Our feelings will not always be right so we have to get a grip of our feelings and trust God. Our behavior is not going to always be just right, so relying on God to teach us better behavior patterns is necessary, as well. Learn from every mistake because God will use them. Character is built by looking back at mistakes you have made and allowing God to show you His way so that you may learn from those mistakes. Those mistakes then become learning experiences. Then you have to die to your own will and press toward being kingdom minded. Character is extremely important in the life of a Christian. Character has to be developed. Please do not overlook the development of true Godly character. Believe God loves you and He is disciplining you for character development. Hebrews 12:11 says:

"For the time being no discipline brings joy, but seems grievous and painful; but afterwards it yields a peaceable fruit of righteousness to those who have been trained by it [a harvest of fruit which consists in righteousness - in conformity to God's will in purpose, thought, and action, resulting in right living and right standing with God."

Along with godly character, you should be very aware of your integrity. Integrity is defined as the quality of being honest and having strong moral principals; moral uprightness. It must be intertwined in godly character. We must not allow a situation we may be experiencing to overshadow our integrity or Godly character. Maintain integrity in every situation you are facing. God wants to know He can trust you. Let integrity be of high priority in your life. Proverbs 11:3 says:

"The integrity of the upright shall guide them:
but the perverseness of transgressors shall destroy them."

Integrity will help guide you to make many decisions when you place high priority on it. It may look like people are getting away with not having integrity about some things, but believe me they are not and God has a way of showing them what moral uprightness is all about. We all have a choice to make decisions based on integrity or just ignore integrity and do what we want to do in order to get results we think we need. I am constantly reminding myself to check my integrity in different situations. It truly keeps me grounded and humble to yield to the will of God. We must die to flesh so that character is built and good integrity is maintained. Checking your integrity will have you to make decisions that may not seem valuable at the time, but press on and do the right thing and God will see that He can trust you. Let integrity aide you in making decisions. The best decision may not be the popular decision, but your integrity will still be intact and you will gain strength.

"The way of the Lord is strength to the upright:
but destruction shall be to the workers of iniquity"
Proverbs 10:29

I think it is important for people to realize that God takes integrity very seriously. There should be more teaching on integrity and godly character. Along with blessings, we have to use the character God teaches us in order to live with integrity or else the blessings will be short lived. As the persecutions arise, do not allow them to make you do things that are not in accordance with godly character and integrity. Believe me, in difficult times when you need to rely on God to show up for you in a very big way, having integrity will keep you and will not allow you to behave the wrong way. Trust God, He brings justice to the just. Psalms 25:21 says:

*"Let integrity and honesty protect me,
for I put my hope in You."*

David was saying that he had done the right things according to
God's standards; therefore he wanted to rely on the fact that he has
used integrity in his dealings with others and God would protect him
in everything he endeavored to accomplish. Integrity goes a long way.
It will bless you and your children. When they experience you behaving
with integrity, they behave the same way. They are being developed by
watching you and are blessed by it.

*"The just man walks in integrity:
his children are blessed after him"*
Proverbs 20:7

This verse makes me sit upright and really consider my ways because
I believe in being good stewards over what God has blessed me to
have and as my children are a blessing from God, I am determined to
steward them well. In that determination, I find that Godly character
and integrity overrides the behavior that is not according to the word of
God. I truly believe living in integrity protects us from backlash of the
bad behavior. God will help you along as you trust Him and let Him
lead you. There will be times when it is easier to not walk in integrity
than to walk in it, but remember God will grace you to do what is right
and strengthen you in the process. When you have peace with God that's
all that matters. Psalms 26:1 says:

*"Judge me, O Lord, for I have trusted also in
the Lord; therefore I shall not slide."*

God is preparing us to be used for His service and in doing that,
persecutions and difficulties will come, floods will rise, afflictions will
be felt, and obstacles will get in the way. I have found the best thing to
do is to not fight it, settle down, and don't run from challenges, but face
them head on in the power of His might and let God deal with them so

that God can use them for your good. Look at them as training for your walk of victory. Don't give up. Stay in the race and fight until the end. God will give you the staying power you need as you continue to go to Him and trust that He is well aware of your plight and He is your very present help. A powerful testimony of many is being able to literally say, "Hey, I'm still here with my integrity intact. I will not give up no matter what. I did not give in and lose my integrity because of the pressures." You know, difficult situations are just that. Yes, they are difficult, but difficult does not mean impossible. There is nothing impossible with God. The question becomes, are you willing to work through the difficulties? Difficulties help you to learn how to maneuver through things to get a desired result. I call it, "Spiritual maneuverability". It involves seeing things differently in order to use those things to increase your ability to maneuver. Use difficulties to teach you how to do things outside of the box for a desired outcome. Sometimes it takes having to read about other inspiring stories of others that had difficulties to go through while reaching for their goals. When you can read or hear about those testimonies, it just gives you a spiritual jolt to continue hoping and pressing. We have to keep moving, we have to continue to oxygenate ourselves with the word of God for the fuel to keep reaching. Just make up your mind to never give up. The woman with the issue of blood had to crawl through a crowd to get healed. David ran from Saul and hid himself in caves until God made him king. Naomi followed Ruth away from her kinsmen. Moses was put along a river as an infant to save his life. Elijah dug two holes and poured water in them to prove God was the only true God. Zacheas climbed a tree. The Shunnamite woman gave her last meal. The disciples left their homes to follow Jesus. Paul was imprisoned, beaten, falsely accused, and hated. Believe me, nothing about those stories were normal. The truth of the matter is that they had to go through those things in order to accomplish God's will. We are encouraged by those stories to believe God and persevere. The power of God is there for all who will decide to push forward through impossible situations.

There will definitely be times of refreshing. You will not always have to go through, but when you do, do what it takes to keep pressing.

Cross the finish line and do it well. Do it with your integrity still intact. It will build and develop godly character. When I think about Paul and how hard it was for him, but he still finished well. He wrote two thirds of the bible, most of which was during the toughest of times. That took some great spiritual stamina. God chose him and I believe God knew what He was doing. I also believe God chose you and He knows what He is doing. God will propel you into victory. You are more than a conqueror. Jesus endured the cross. He also endured all night beatings. He endured Calvary.

"For you are in need of endurance, so that after you have done the will of God, you will receive the promise"
2 Timothy 10:36

There is a promise. There is a reward in it for you and it is not just in the sweet by and by. It is here on earth, while you wait on the sweet by and by. I don't know about you, but I want my reward and I plan on enjoying it. Don't allow the persecutions to get you so uptight that you can't enjoy the victory. Shout with a voice of triumph, shout with a voice of praise, shout with a voice of triumph. You are victorious.

Living a godly life and doing the will of God is so much more than being persecuted. We really enjoy great benefits. There are others that need to see your victory, that need to hear of your victory, and that need to be encouraged going through as they experience your triumph. Take courage in knowing God is with you to deliver you. There will be times when you will have to encourage yourself in the Lord. God makes it so. That is true maturity when you don't have to have someone cheering you on all the time because there will be times when you will not have that and you will have to trust God and move out on His marching orders with or without a cheering squad or even one cheerleader. Believe me, sometimes you will have to be your own cheerleader. I think God really loves that because it shows true trust. I can see Him saying, "Look at him/her, yes that's the spirit. I want to be reminded of my word to perform it." I don't know about you, but when I know God Almighty is my advocate, I gain strength and determination to keep doing what He told me to do and I can stand through adversity. Romans 8:31 says:

> *"What then shall we say to [all] this? If God is for us, who [can be] against us? [Who can be our foe, if God is on our side?]."*

What powerful security it is, when you are assured of God being in your corner. God told me one day when I felt so alone and abandoned that with Him I am the majority. You don't have to look for a voice of agreement when you know you have heard from God and He is on your side. Just keep pressing and soon your goal will be accomplished. Keep getting up even though you may get knocked down several times. Never give up. Decide over and over again to be determined to relentlessly press. Always go to God for your strength. Of course you will get weak, of course you will get discouraged, of course you will feel let down at times, of course you will feel like no one understands, of course things will get heavy, of course obstacles will be there to hinder you, but no matter what comes always remember to go to God for strength. I believe God purposely removes people from our lives at times because He knows we depend on people too much and on Him too little. Our strength comes from God and Him alone. God is our source for everything. He will send you resources, but He is the Source. God will certainly use individuals along the way to help you as resources, but your ultimate help is from God.

In 1 Thessalonians 3:3-5, Paul explains clearly:

> *"That no one [of you] should be disturbed and beguiled and led astray by these afflictions and difficulties [to which I have referred]. For you yourselves know that this is [unavoidable in our position, and must be recognized as] our appointed lot. For even when we were with you, [you know] we warned you plainly beforehand that we were to be pressed with difficulties and made to suffer affliction, just as to your own knowledge it has [since] happened. That is*

the reason that, when I could bear [the suspense] no longer,
I sent that I might learn [how you were standing the strain
and the endurance of] your faith, [for I was fearful] lest
somehow the tempter had tempted you and our toil [among
you should prove to] be fruitless and to no purpose."

There is a Divine purpose for what you have to go through as you complete God's assignment for your life. Paul is explaining that he was concerned about us giving up due to the many troubles, trials, and tribulations (the 3 T's). He was concerned that the afflictions also may contribute to us giving up and I do admit it gets very hard not to give up sometimes, but God always comes through with the right thing needed at the right time. We just have to stay tuned to God's channel. Channel in on God's power. Paul here was basically encouraging the Thessalonians to remain stable and to not allow difficulties to intimidate them. God does not want us to let evil situations move us. Can you stand the strain? Do not be impressed by difficult circumstances. God can trump anything the enemy does. Nothing is more powerful than God, so do not be moved by the enemy. Just say to yourself, "I am more than a conqueror, this will pass, life happens and I am still victorious." Don't be impressed by it all, it's nothing compared to the power of God. God always has a way of escape. He always has a better plan than the enemy. God can circumvent anything the enemy tries to throw your way. Stay encouraged by focusing on God and not the issue. Try your best to waste as less time as possible focusing on the issue. This will enable you to get the divine strategy to overcome because you already know that you are an overcomer. Do not allow the pressure to push you back. Press through the pressure and gain stronger spiritual muscles and maneuverability. The blessing is in the pressing. I plead the blood of Jesus over you. Keep going. You will have a powerful testimony and your onlookers will be encouraged as well. Well let me correct myself here, not all of them. Some of them will be proven wrong. Rely on all the teaching you have had in scripture. Some of it was for the present time, but some of your teaching is for future reference. Always refer back to what you have been taught in the word or if you haven't been taught, then allow the Holy Spirit to teach you and take you through scripture to teach you how to stay strong and remain stable in the midst of difficult circumstances. The treasure God has blessed you with is worth it. Begin to start quoting scripture over and over again until faith comes and you are convinced of the truth and I press through to trust God. This will completely confuse the enemy. The thoughts that he is giving you are not what you are saying and he cannot stand that. The truth of the matter is that it will turn out for the glory of God when you completely trust Him and depend on Gods timing and effort to see you through.

Paul illuminates in Philippians 1:12-14:

> *"Now I want you to know and continue to rest assured,*
> *brethren, that what [has happened] to me [this imprisonment]*
> *has actually only served to advance and give a renewed*
> *impetus to the [spreading of the] good news (the Gospel).*
> *So much is this a fact that throughout the whole imperial*
> *guard and to all the rest [here] my imprisonment had*
> *become generally known to be in Christ [that I am a*
> *prisoner in His service and for Him]. And [also] most of*
> *the brethren have derived fresh confidence in the Lord*
> *because of my chains and are much more bold to speak*
> *and publish fearlessly the Word of God [acting with*
> *more freedom and indifference to the consequences]."*

I think Paul was laughing when he said this. Just think about it. I think he could have been tickled pink at the enemy. What a kick in the teeth for the enemy to see that what he meant for evil, God turned around for your good. That is the ultimate victory. You won't just come out smelling clean, but you will gain a better witness, strength, and whatever else God decides to give you through it. It is a platform for God's glory to shine. All the onlookers will begin to see how God moved on your behalf and how they too can overcome adversity as they learn to depend on God and trust that God will take care of them through it all. I love it. Listen, Paul didn't get offended and stop. He kept pushing, pressing, and moving. Offense will stifle you and make you paranoid. Proverbs 18:19 says:

"A brother offended is harder to be won over than a strong city, and [their] contentions separate them like bars of a castle."

Paul did not waste precious time on offense. He would have had to go through all the turmoil of getting himself back together and bringing walls down in order to do the will of God. That's how we should be. We should understand that offenses will come, but we don't have to take them. When someone gives offense. Don't take it. It's as if I were giving you a ticking time bomb. Would you take it? You sure wouldn't take it. That is how we should treat offense. Try your very best to not take offense or get rid of it as soon as possible because it is an absolute waste of precious time and effort. Nothing good comes out of offense for the giver or the receiver. I have made up my mind to just have God to deal with my offenders. That way He can make sure they are learning a lesson from making trouble for others. God will make sure of that. I have to pray for God to really cleanse my heart so that it can remain pure and free of offense. We win every time that way.

We can win in such a sweet way that the devil is punch-drunk. Like he was when Jesus rose, Paul got saved and wrote one third of the New Testament, Joseph was set free and put in charge and saved the Israelites, Moses was not killed as a baby and set the captives free, David escaped Saul and reigned as king, Esther was appointed queen and saved the Jews from death, and so forth and so on. Awesome testimonies. You too can have so many awesome testimonies. Sure, they all had difficulties, but they persevered for purpose. Our purpose is not just about us. It's about the others we were sent here to help. It helps others to see you persevere. Somehow, it gives them strength as well. The glory of God will shine brighter than ever in your life. Romans 8:18 says:

"For I reckon that the sufferings of this present time are not worthy to be compared with the glory which shall be revealed in us."

CHAPTER 5

LIVING IN HARMONY WITH PEACE

"And let the peace (soul harmony which comes)
from Christ rule (act as umpire continually) in your hearts
[deciding and settling with finality all questions that arise
in your minds, in that peaceful state] to which as members
of Christ's] one body you were also called [to live]. And be
thankful (appreciative), [giving praise to God always]"
Col 3:15

We must allow peace to have free reign (be in control) in order to rule in our hearts. As peace rules and has total control, we will govern our lives according to that principle. Peace is our protection and a barrier for us in times of adversity. Peace is so important to living a life full of God's power. It should be prevalent in the life of every Christian. First, be at peace with yourself. I make it a point to make sure I give everything that may rob me of peace to God so that the enemy will back down on his tactics to keep those things on my mind. Sometimes I have to say "Wait a minute, this is taking up too much time and space in my thought life and I bind all mind binding spirits, in the name of Jesus." Then I loose the blood of Jesus over my mind and focus on scripture or any thing that is praiseworthy. After that I start praising God. I begin to feel refreshed and motivated to do something great for the kingdom. Philippians 4:6-7 says, *"Do not fret or have any anxiety about anything, but in every circumstance and in everything, by prayer and petition (definite requests), with thanksgiving, continue to make your wants known to God. And God's peace [shall be yours, that tranquil state of a soul assured of its salvation through Christ, and so fearing nothing from God and being content with its earthly lot of whatever sort that is, that peace] which transcends all understanding shall garrison and mount guard over your hearts and minds in Christ Jesus."* This scripture speaks of an assurance that Gods peace gives us. It is a security that is well guarded by the power of God. Living the godly life should command peace. Turmoil is not an atmosphere that you can effectively hear from God and live a life accomplishing God's will. Where there is confusion, God's will is frustrated and off track. 1 Corinthians 14:33 says, *"For God is not the author of confusion, but of peace, as in all churches of the saints."* Peace helps to keep stable you during uncertain or unstable situations. By that I mean it keeps you grounded. It allows you to let go and let God. Peace is defined as a state of quiet tranquility, freedom from disturbance or agitation. I look at peace as a place of rest in your spirit, mind, and body. When you are not at peace your body goes through changes internally and externally. It really is a place you can go to in the midst of turmoil. Picture yourself leaving confusion and moving into a place that is void of agitating circumstances. You can actually do that physically, mentally, and spiritually. Sometimes it takes removing yourself physically in order to experience the mental and spiritual peace you need. Sometimes just getting away will create the atmosphere needed to allow you to have that calm needed to gather things in perspective. You can mentally leave a place of confusion as well and still be there physically, but mentally and spiritually be far away in the presence of God. There are times when you cannot get away, but you can allow God to help you drown out everything that creates confusion and focus on Him. That's one of the reasons why we have imaginations. When I get alone with God and allow Him to speak to me, His voice gets louder and other voices fade into insignificance. Peace and the Holy Spirit should flow together. The Holy Spirit is our counselor. Being filled with the Holy Spirit is so important to our walk with God and making decisions in our lives. We should not overlook the presence of the Holy

Spirit in our lives. The presence of the Holy Spirit is crucial to being in and accomplishing the will of God in our lives. Peace should be what helps you know that you have heard from God on an issue that you have prayed about. When peace is not present, then wait until you obtain peace before making any moves. Allow the Holy Spirit to lead you to the decision of peace. Now just because you have peace in doing something does not mean it will not require faith. God expects us to take steps of faith and have peace with the decision we make. Peace is not some comfortable state that does not require faith. Peace is saying, although it may be hard and uncomfortable, I have peace in what I am doing. It's a place of rest that God gives you in the midst of tough situations. It gives you that inner strength to let you know that you can do what God tells you to do against all odds. Even though it's a step of faith, you have peace with it.

Moses had a tough assignment, but he allowed God to give him step-by-step instruction on how to free the Israelites. His task seemed impossible to man. His task would have been impossible on his own, but his assignment was divine and God gave him divine power and strategy. When he went to Pharaoh he knew the king would not humble himself and submit to the will of God. He knew Pharaoh would fight him tooth and nail. Now let's take a look at this carefully. Two men, Moses and his brother, went to the king of Egypt, who had a mass army at his disposal and told him that God said to free the Israelites from slavery. Of course, the king would be furious. Of course the king would flex his muscles and laugh Moses right out of the castle. Instead of Moses giving in to what he saw, because he had peace with what God told him to do, he pressed through and relied on God to bring down one of the most powerful kings at that time along with his kingdom. Moses was chosen to do the impossible, primarily to show that God is All-powerful and no foe can withstand Him.

> *"And the Egyptians shall know that I am the Lord,*
> *when I have gotten me honor upon Pharaoh, and all*
> *his host, upon his chariots, and upon his horsemen"*
> Exodus 14:20

Can you just use your imagination here and see what Moses was up against. That had to have been extremely stressful. I have to admit that I probably would have been awestruck at that particular task given by God against Pharoah and his great army. God chose Moses because He knew he had been brought up around the kings Palace and would not be so intimidated by what he saw. I'm sure that when the guards saw him they were a little nervous about doing anything to him considering who he was and how they remember him being brought up in the Palace as one of Pharoah's own sons. Moses had peace about what he was doing and he kept his peace even when Pharoah tried to intimidate him. Peace guarded his heart and his mind and kept him stable.

Peace keeps you from moving when your heart and mind wants to fail you and take flight trying to take things in your own hands to make something happen. It helps you to rest in the power of God. Peace is submission to the power and will of God. It brings resolve, no matter the cost. Peace elevates your thinking to Gods thinking. Peace places all the work on God, but the obedience on you. It may be tough, but our God is tougher. I wholeheartedly believe that peace is crucial to a blessed life in Christ because it keeps us sane, stable, and trusting in God. Along your path, God will lead you through scripture to confirm what He has assigned you to do. He will give you the tenacity and determination to remain stable through your decisions even when others disagree or do not understand what God is doing in your life. Sometimes you can't explain or understand what God is doing in your life, but it's imperative that you are in a state of peace as you continue on in Him. I use to worry a lot. I made it a habit of finding something to worry about. I chose to worry over peace because I thought that would make God move somehow, but it only made matters worse. It also made me think that I could do something to help. I would mull the thing over and over in my head to try and see what should I do. I never stopped to think that God would take care of it for me. I had to learn to cast all my cares on him. Have you been doing what I used to do? You may not call it worry, but that is exactly what it is. I never admitted to worrying, but I was doing just that by thinking about it all the time and trying to determine what I should be doing about the situation. I worried about everything, the kids, my marriage, the finances, my future, my job, my relationship with my siblings. You name it. I worried about it. I am so thankful for my loving Savior who saved me from a life of worry or should I say the bondage of worry. He took me on a journey one day through scripture that I will share with you. He gently led me in His presence and started to speak sweet nothings in my ear. I remember it like it was yesterday. He led me to 1 Peter 5:7:

> *"Casting the whole of your care [all your anxieties, all your worries, all your concerns, once and for all] on Him, for He cares for you affectionately and cares about you watchfully."*

He then showed me to Psalm 55:22:

> *"Cast your burden on the Lord [releasing the weight of it] and He will sustain you; He will never allow the [consistently] righteous to be moved (made to slip, fall, or fail)."*

We then went to Psalm 168:8a:

> *"The Lord will perfect that which concerns me."*

God also took me to Matthew 6:26-27 that says:

> *"Look at the birds of the air; they neither sow nor reap nor gather into barns, and yet your heavenly Father keeps feeding them. Are you not worth much more than they? And who by worrying and being anxious can add one unit of measure (cubit) to his stature or to the span of his life?"*

I read all of Matthew chapter six and just sat in His presence. I felt the warmth of His touch in my heart and mind. Everything within me settled down into the pillow of His arms and I knew I was in His presence at that moment. I had been in such turmoil and discontentment before He led me away to that place of peace in His presence. My Father took me on a walk with Him through the coolness of His word to talk with me and give me exactly what I needed. I felt like a little child holding my Fathers hand as we walked. As I sat and meditated, I reflected on His love for me once again. You must understand that I had formed a bad habit that God had to stop. The worry cycle I had created within myself was going to be used by the enemy to destroy me. I'm glad God caught me when He did because I would have wrinkled a lot faster, my health would have started to fail me in numerous ways just because I was worrying too much. When we worry, it's like taking poison. That's what God told me. He said, "I want you free of that poison, I love you too much to just let that happen to you, my love." I felt like I was on top of the world at that moment. His love engulfed me and I just meditated on it. I memorized the scriptures and said them over and over until they stuck in my spirit and I yielded to them. I still say them over and over to keep the enemy under my feet. Every time that habit tries to sneak up on me again, I resist the enemy at the onset and start quoting the scriptures God gave me in order to overcome it.

John 14:27 says:

> *"Peace I leave with you; My [own] peace I now give and bequeath to you. Not as the world gives do I give to you. Do not let your hearts be troubled, neither let them be afraid. [Stop allowing yourselves to be agitated and disturbed; and do not permit yourselves to be fearful and intimidated and cowardly and unsettled.]"*

It is very apparent here that Jesus has provided us with His special peace, and we must appropriate His peace in our lives and not let our hearts be troubled or afraid. We have to pursue, with all diligence a place of peace in all that we encounter because that is where God is flowing. I never want to be where God is not flowing, so when I find confusion in my life I quickly start to look carefully at my present circumstances in order to find peace. I literally have to leave the physical area sometimes in order to pursue the spiritual and mental area of peace. This act of finding peace allows us to avoid experiencing those things that the enemy puts in our way to agitate and intimidate us. The enemy brings fear so he can torment us and bring us out of our peace, but we have to be determined not to let him. I used to wake up night after night with thoughts of fear and torment. Things the enemy would tell me to cloud my thinking and make me come out of my peace and act on what he was telling me. In the quiet darkness, the enemy spoke as if he was standing right in front of me. I felt so much fear and agitation in my heart. Until one night I rebuked his stupid bottom as I stood up to him and told him I bind you and these evil thoughts in the name of Jesus and whatever I bind on earth is bound in heaven and whatever I loose on earth is loosed in heaven. I took authority over my thoughts. I loosed the blood of Jesus over my mind and heart and prayed for complete peace. After that I heard God whisper in my ear so gently and sweetly, "Let not your heart be troubled, neither let it be afraid." Boy did my heart settle. I felt His whisper in my heart and it felt like warm tea resting within me. My head rested ever so softly on my pillow and I went to sleep in peace with a smile on my face. Right now, if you have something that is really bothering you that the enemy reminds you of consistently throughout the day, and at night he really gets busy trying to torment you and rob you of sleep and peace, please understand that you have the power to put a stop to it. Rebuke him and receive God's peace. Let not your heart be troubled, neither let it be afraid. You see, after I received God's love then I could readily receive His peace. God began giving me answers. He was able to come in and arrest my thinking and give me the right thoughts that were according to His word. On a continual basis we must yield to what God is saying and drown out all the other distractions that come to lead us astray.

You have to be adamant about refusing to live in turmoil. Turmoil is used by the enemy to keep you distracted and out of the will of God. Where there is turmoil, there is darkness. Light does not tolerate darkness. Light does away with darkness immediately. Light has no conversation with darkness and to be quite frank, darkness has nothing much to say to light because it knows it has to leave when true light shows up. John 3:20-21 says:

"For every wrongdoer hates (loathes, detests) the Light, and will not come out into the Light but shrinks from it, lest his works (his deeds, his activities, his conduct) be exposed and reproved. But he who practices truth [who does what is right] comes out into the Light; so that his works may be plainly shown to be what they are—wrought with God [divinely prompted, done with God's help, in dependence upon Him]."

When people avoid you, be assured they are walking in darkness and your light exposes their deeds thus, they would rather avoid the light you carry rather than be exposed. Now if it's you, on the other hand avoiding someone else, please expose all darkness and let God come in and shed light on your attitude and the situation. It's okay, just admit the thing and move forward in light and peace. There are so many times I have been in darkness and God had to shed light on my behavior. I then had to be honest with myself as God revealed some things to me and let the Holy Spirit lead me to the light. When my husband and I would argue about things that I thought I was right about, I would be adamant about getting my point across. Then afterward the Holy Spirit would enlighten me on my behavior and lead me to right behavior. Then I had to go and get it right. I had to go and apologize to shed light on the situation, therefore darkness had to flee. Peace had to be restored. Also, there are times when I would be led by God to apologize even when I thought I was right. You see, the issue wasn't whether I was right or wrong, it was to restore peace no matter what. I believe peace is the ultimate state of being God wants us to live in. That doesn't mean the type of peace that puts us in La La Land whisping through the wheat fields, as we flow through life light as a feather. Yes, there are times when you are going to have to confront some things and get things right. There will be times that you have to make up your mind to do the will of God, even if others are not at peace with your decision. What it means is having peace of mind on all the decisions you have to make. Being at peace with your decision and sticking with it. Being still in the midst of a storm after you have given it to God is what I mean. Going through tough times with a sense of ease within, rooted and grounded in God's love and concern for you and your situation. Shaping your thoughts around the word of God. Your mind has a tendency to shape your words. Be careful to weigh what you are thinking about and do not let it escape to your words unless it is what you want to see happen. We will be better off to think like Philippians 4:8 says:

"For the rest brethren, whatever is true, whatever is worthy of reverence and is honorable and seemly, whatever is just, whatever is pure, whatever is lovely, and lovable, whatever is kind and winsome and gracious, if there is any virtue and excellence, if there is anything worthy of praise, think on and weigh and take account of these things [fix your minds on them]."

Take the time to meditate on that scripture so it can take you to the things God wants you to think about. Please don't allow your mind to contradict what God says. Your mind must be in agreement with the word of God. Speak the word of God over your mind daily. The scripture says to focus on whatever is true. The word of God is the truth. Focus on what you know for sure. Focus on the good things that are happening around you. It could be the new day God has given you, a smile on the face of your child, the health of your body, or anything that will keep you from being negative in your thinking. Always be very aware of what you are thinking about. Maintain peace in your mind. You will find yourself fighting to maintain peace of mind as you step out on faith to what God has for you to do in life. I often find myself praying over my mind and declaring that I have the mind of Christ and also that I have a sound mind.

The faith steps will come to you as you take one at a time. When you find yourself at a stand still, it is all right to stand still. This will enable you to hear from God for your next step of faith. I emphasize "steps of faith" because all along as you hear from God, you will need to trust him and have peace with your decision to step out on what it is He is asking of you. The journey will not be easy, neither will it be all smooth sailing at times, but the peace will be there and that is the key, His peace.

Yes, you will make mistakes. Yes, you will fail at some things. Yes, you will be discouraged, but get back up. Wipe yourself off and get back into the flow of things. It's ok to make mistakes, just be careful to learn from every mistake. Sit and ask God what is it that you should learn from each mistake. Mistakes build character when you learn from them. You will find peace within when you are okay when making mistakes. Peace will overwhelm any feeling of condemnation and evil thoughts about yourself that the enemy tries to give you. You will be able to rest in the peace of God. Rest is a powerful place to be in God. When we rest in God, we rest in His grace and all He has promised us. Rest in the promises of God from this point on. As you speak the promises over every situation be assured that in Christ is a good place to rest.

Peace in God involves trust in God. It requires us to be still and know that He is God. It completes every scenario the enemy sends your way with the simple fact that you trust God wholly. Proverbs 3:5-6 says:

"Trust in the Lord with all your heart and lean not unto your own understanding, but in all your ways acknowledge Him and He will direct your path."

Trusting and waiting on God to move isn't easy without peace. To be honest, even with peace it's a stretch, but it is a part of the process. You must fill your heart and mind with positive confessions about the situation in accordance with the word of God. Thank Him for working on your behalf. Believe He loves you and is very aware of everything involved with you. Stay focused on Him and be vigilant not to listen to anything the enemy says. Be diligent to seek Gods presence in order to remain in peace. God's presence is peaceful and completely tranquil that you may have rest in your spirit. There has been so many times the enemy have tried to pull me out of the peace of God by bombarding my mind with thoughts and statements that are just not true. God said to me one day, "Trust Me, emphasis on Me, emphasis Mine." That completely blew me away. I just sat there saying, "Thank you Jesus," because I knew it was Him coming to settle my spirit into trusting Him and not what I saw.

My husband is one of the most peaceful people I know. He is a very humble man of God and he knows how to hold his peace. I see him filling his mind and heart with the word of God quite frequently, which encourages me to want to follow. He believes God over the enemy and says that he is determined to fill his spirit and mind with God's word over what the enemy is trying to say to him or do to him. He uses the word on his mind to keep himself from adhering to whatever the enemy is up to. I used to think him strange for always wanting the word spoken to him and in his ear as he agrees with it, but after understanding the strategy to keep the devil under his feet, I follow his lead. I am amazed at the times he could have said so many things to people after they have done him wrong, but he kept his peace because he completely trusted God to handle it. Isaiah 26:3-4 says:

> *"You will guard him and keep him in perfect and constant peace whose mind [both its inclination and its character] is stayed on You, because he commits himself to You, leans on You, and hopes confidently in You. So trust in the Lord (commit yourself to Him, lean on Him, hope confidently in Him) forever; for the Lord God is an everlasting Rock [the Rock of ages]."*

Everything we give to God is God's to handle. It is no longer ours, so do not take it back when the pressure is on. We then need to lean on Him. We have to trust God's timing and ability to do what is right at the right time. That was a big one to get over for me because I was so accustomed to handling my own struggles. When God started to teach me true trust in Him. I flunked every test imaginable. I was so ready to take care of everything on my own that I didn't even give God the chance to do anything. I didn't even pray for His help. I just proceeded to do whatever I thought was necessary to make things the way I thought they should be when God all the while was sitting back watching me patiently and waiting on me to trust Him. When you trust God, you really do have peace. You won't be bothered by things the enemy sends to rob you of your peace. You will have a state of mind that will not be taken away to a state of confusion. It will not sit well with you to be bothered so much by a thing. You spirit man will identify to you that you are not in peace and you need to do what it takes to gather your peace back. I find myself thanking God in the midst of hard times to maintain peace. Sometimes I get out and help others that I may maintain a state of peace. There are times that I quote the word over and over again until peace comes. I absolutely refuse to give up my peace.

CHAPTER 6

NEVER GIVE UP

This may be one of the most frequent things you encounter as you discover who you are and what God has designed for you to do on earth because as you make your mind and heart up to agree with God and move accordingly in harmony with God, the enemy will try to set up blockades and distractions. The idea of giving up seems so easy many times, but I encourage you to stay firm, be steadfast, and allow God to be your strength in every weakness. As you move in harmony with Gods will for your life, God will be there to lean on and hold you up as necessary. There will be times when it seems nothing is going right. There will be times that make you want to literally throw in the towel and be done with it all. You will have justifying reasons to just give up, but don't do it. Stay in the fight. God will give you what I call "staying power." Whatever it takes to remain stable and keep moving, God will give it to you. As you call on Him, you will find much assurance and encouragement. Whatever obstacles you may have in your life right now, please take this encouragement to go through them and not give up! Though it may be difficult at times, never give up. Habakkuk 3:17-19 says:

> *"Though the fig tree does not blossom and there is no fruit on the vines, [though] the product of the olive fails and the fields yield no food, though the flock is cut off from the fold and there are no cattle in the stalls, Yet I will rejoice in the Lord; I will exult in the [victorious] God of my salvation! The Lord God is my Strength, my personal bravery, and my invincible army; He makes my feet like*

hinds' feet and will make me to walk [not to stand still in terror, but to walk] and make [spiritual] progress upon my high places [of trouble, suffering, or responsibility]!"

We should allow our difficulties to help us develop "hinds' feet." When a deer senses trouble, it does not stand still in terror and quit, no, quite to the contrary, it takes off using primarily its hind legs to run faster. When we have hind's feet, we will not allow terror to make us stand still terrified in the midst of our problems. Instead, we will walk and make continual progress through our trouble, suffering, responsibility, or whatever it is that's trying to hold us back and make us quit. Hard times will make it so easy to quit, but God is closer to you than you may think in those hard times. There are countless times I feel like giving up and that feeling is so strong, it's hard to contain, but then God comes in and reminds me of His love and continual support. In those times it is imperative that we get in Gods presence because God knows exactly the right button to push to get us back on track. God is the ultimate encourager. After God shows up and comforts or do what it takes to confirm me again, then I find it hard to quit. Yes, that's right God comes in and turns the whole thing around and makes it difficult to quit. It's easy to give up in hard times; it takes faith and trust to go through those difficult times. Your faith will be strengthened through your hard times. Know that God wants to be with you and encourage you to push through and keep going through the storms of life. I want to impart deep within your spirit a power given to me by God for you to possess deep within you to not give up. You may ask, "How do I continue believing God for the promise"? You have to keep speaking it out and keeping it alive within you. Do not live by what you see in the natural, but live by what you say. Say what you see in the spiritual realm. You will begin to get back on track as you begin to see things differently. Sometimes a different perspective is all it takes to keep on keeping on. Daily speaking Gods' promises transforms your mind into the mind of Christ. Jesus Christ is the Word and the word of God is His promises; therefore, as you speak the word, you transform your mind into the mind of Christ. This will help you endure as the scripture says in Hebrews 10:36:

"For you have need of steadfast patience and endurance,
so that you may perform and fully accomplish
the will of God, and thus receive and carry away
[and enjoy to the full] what is promised."

Great endurance is necessary for the promise to be fulfilled. One thing I must say is that you will enjoy doing what you were created to do, which does help in hard times as well. Your passion and drive will be strong concerning your true purpose and you will definitely have peace of mind while doing it.

There is an eager expectation waiting for you to speak life to it. Are you quoting the word of God daily over yourself? When you habitually do that, it will help you endure through the toughest of times. It will also help when people come to you and speak contrary to the word of God over your life because the word will well up inside you and rebuke that which was spoken. Be vigilant and relentless as you pursue the will of God and His purpose will prevail. Always stay hungry for God's power to bring the enemy and his tactics to his knees. As Joel 2:21 says:

"Fear not O land; be glad and rejoice,
for the Lord has done great things."

God will do the difficult things that you cannot handle. Give God praise in the most difficult times and see the salvation of the Lord. God is eagerly waiting on the opportunity to be that strong tower that the enemy cannot withstand. When things get hard, don't sit down, stand up and have confidence in the God we serve. Stand up, take authority over the enemy, and release the power of God on the situation. Stand up and take authority over your feelings and declare the Word of God. You confuse the enemy when you stand up in the midst of adversity. When you don't bow your head in shame when he comes against you, he gets bewildered. Your standing, your praising, and your smiling will defeat every plan of the enemy. When you continue to be encouraged in the midst of all the enemy tries to throw at you and know God will always come to your rescue, you confuse and defeat the enemy. That is prime opportunity for God to show you that with Him on your side, you are the majority. Joel 2:27 says:

> *"And you shall know, understand, and realize that I am in the midst of Israel and that I the Lord am your God and there is none else. My people shall never be put to shame."*

Never hang your head in shame. Wait to see God move in His perfect timing. Do not be concerned about how much time it's taking. God is eternity and He holds time in His hands for His perfect timing to take place in your life. I had to learn this the hard way. I had to bump my head a few times to understand that although God has shown me something, it may not happen right away and trying to make it happen out of His timing is not going to yield God's results.

Become captivated and engulfed in hope. Let hope continue to be alive within you. Be a prisoner of hope. Zechariah 9:12 says:

> *"Return to the stronghold [of security and prosperity], you prisoner of hope; even today do I declare that I will restore double your former prosperity to you."*

Our attitude must be that of hope because it has a lot to do with how God works in our lives. When we decide to trust God's word and never give up, we will have victory. God said He will restore double. Hope gives you a positive attitude no matter what things are looking like. Hope is expecting something good is going to happen in your life everyday. God wants us to be prisoners of hope and believe He can change anything that needs to be changed and with God's help we can do whatever that needs to be done. We all can fulfill Gods purpose for our lives by living expectantly in hope and being passionate for the things God is passionate about. Hope keeps you in times of trouble. It keeps your heart strong when it wants to throw in the towel through hard times. Proverbs 13:12 teaches us:

> *"Hope deferred makes the heart sick, but when*
> *the desire is fulfilled, it is a tree of life."*

Hope deferred is disappointment. Do not allow disappointment to stifle you, instead turn your disappointment into a reappointment by allowing God to show you what to do at that particular time until your breakthrough or as the scripture above says, the desire is fulfilled. I am going to refer again to the experience I used earlier in your reading in which God told me one day when I felt so disappointed and let down to call three people, not to converse with them, but to just encourage them, show them some love and then say goodbye. I remember thinking, but I need to be encouraged. My heart is so heavy right now, how can I encourage them? Nevertheless, I allowed God's grace to enable me to obey the prompting of the Holy Spirit and carried out what God said to do. Once I did it, oh my goodness, it sparked a new fire in me. Each phone call encouraged me more and more. I began doing everything I needed to do to continue to pursue what that disappointment came to interrupt. It sparked new hope inside of me and I began to praise God. Three people represented the Father, Son, and the Holy Spirit and I knew I had all three in my corner cheering me on to keep it moving. God quickly moved me from disappointment to reappointment because He gave me fresh ideas and a new outlook as He rekindled my heart with the words of encouragement I used to encourage the three people I called. It completely changed my way of thinking about the situation. When you are assured that God is for you, you will allow Him to give you fresh insight and you will act on that insight. Psalms 138:8 says:

> *"The Lord will perfect that which concerns me;*
> *Your mercy and loving-kindness, O Lord, endure*
> *forever, forsake not the works of Your own hands."*

As God leads you to complete His work, He is invisibly moving through you and He won't let you fail.

Hope fits in the space of time that is between what circumstances are saying and what your spirit knows is true from the Word of God. It occupies the space between the promise and the fulfillment of it. No matter what your circumstances look like or what people are saying, hang in there. Help is on the way. The harder it gets, the closer your help is. I'm reminded of this steep hill close to my house God had me to run, and I do emphasize God told me to run it because I had no intentions to run up that long, curvy, and very steep hill. It seemed like the more I ran the steeper it got. I remember thinking, what in the world was I thinking. Maybe God didn't tell me to do this. Do those statements sound familiar? As I was running it and wanting to give up and stop, I heard God say to me, "The steeper it gets, the closer you're getting to the end." Then God took me up in the spirit and said to me, "Now think about that spiritually and conclude that the harder it gets, the closer you are to the promise." That completely changed my perspective about that hill, I would like to say it made it easier, but I must admit it didn't. I'm telling you I felt like the little engine that could. It was still hard, but I knew I could do it and I began to think about the grace of God and call on His grace to help me to make it. That's what we all need to do, call on God's grace, which is fully sufficient. I had to stay positive and encourage myself that God's grace is what I need to do what God told me to do. As I began to call on the grace of God, He reminded me to stay focused on the promise and keep it moving, even if it's just a little at a time. Those curves on the hill made it hard to see the end, but hope helps us to keep it moving when we cannot see the end. Romans 8:24-25 confirms:

"For in [this] hope we were saved. But hope [the object of], which is seen, is not hope. For how can one hope for what he already sees? But if we hope for what is still unseen by us, we wait for it with patience and composure."

Waiting for it with patience and composure means to wait for it with a good attitude so that we won't break down and lose heart along the way. Choosing to trust God no matter what it looks like and learning to accept what we don't understand are two attitudes that help us remain hopeful when we are in the process of waiting. Jeremiah 17:7 says:

"[Most] blessed is the man who believes in, trusts in, and relies on the Lord, and whose hope and confidence the Lord is."

Hope helps us continue to take steps of faith. Hope helps our attitude to remain positive. Hope helps our thinking to be renewed. Hope activates our creativity and gives us zeal and energy. Hope turns the light on in dark places and dark times in our lives. It keeps you on your toes, alert, expectant, and always on ready for the new possibilities. It also helps you to think outside the box. It broadens your perspective and allows God to show you new ways of doing things. Keep your thoughts hopeful, completely filled with hope and things will eventually change. Romans 5:2 explains:

"Because of our faith, Christ has brought us into this place of undeserved privilege where we now stand, and we confidently and joyfully look forward to sharing God's glory. "

The promises of God are there for you and me to increase our hope. Never give up hope in the purpose for your life. Always have a can-do, too-easy mentality. Don't quit on God, He'll never quit on you. I declare and decree that you are going to be everything God created you to be.

If we move in childlike trust to obey what we believe God has told us to do, even if that decision is wrong, God will take that mistake and work it out for our good. The reason this is true is because Romans 8:28 states that:

"All things work together and fit into God's plan for good for those of us who are called according to His purpose."

God has a powerful purpose for your life and keeping hope strong within you is going to get you there. Not shying away from making a mistake. Mistakes are going to happen, but trust God through them and learn what you can through them. Being afraid to be wrong is a form of pride believe it or not. I went through that numerous times and decided that so what if I'm wrong. I'll recover if I don't let pride hinder me from admitting it and getting what I can from the mistake and wiping the dust off and getting up and back into it.

Be determined not to give up no matter what. Jesus Christ in us gives us the determination we need to pursue our dreams and not be afraid to set goals. If you don't set goals, then your dreams will never be more than just dreams, but when you set goals and set out to accomplish them, you are working toward those dreams coming true. Your dreams are not going to just fall out of the sky. I was always afraid to set goals because I always thought I would mess up something along the way and not be able to make them come to fruition, but when Jesus came into my heart, He let me know I was capable of pursuing my dreams and setting goals and that He was there to enable me to complete them. I think back on how my mom raised ten kids on her own without a husband there to help support us. She was determined to allow us to live in a nice, loving home with nice things and that hard work would pay off.

She purposefully made it her aim to work hard and do the right things to provide for us. There wasn't a holiday that we did not have something new to wear on that day. She always bought at least two outfits each. It was fun to just get up and have something new to put on for the holiday. We loved it. Although we did not have the best of everything, she did her best to give us what she could afford. She was very organized with her spending. She knew what she wanted and did not depend on man to give it to her. She depended on God. She taught us to respect and reverence God. She woke up every morning at 4:30 a.m., with a song by Andre Crouch called, "The blood will never lose its power" and I can remember thinking to myself so many mornings, "Oh no there she goes with that song again." Little did I know that that was her way of getting herself ready in her spirit for that day. That song helped her to get into the presence of God. That song gave her strength to go on when times were getting hard, and God used it to give her that extra push of strength early in the morning that she needed to keep going. It also gave her courage when she felt discouraged. When I sing that song now, my heart can still hear her sing it and I get it now. I truly do.

The effort and time she put into talking to us and encouraging us was priceless. We always enjoyed talking to mama. She taught us so much during those talks. She would make us laugh as she taught us important things about life. She taught us to have respect for others. She taught us and also demonstrated to us a great work ethic. She imparted tremendous wisdom to us. I am still reminded of the things she taught us to this day. She taught us to love and enjoy working hard to get what you want. She taught us to be independent of man. She was funny, smart, and very intuitive. She was faced with having to raise all ten of us after my father died, but mama never gave up hope and she also just plain never gave up. She was determined not to send us off to different family members for them to raise us.

By the grace of God, she did it. She kept us together and raised us in one home. As I reflect back, I remember the tough times, but more importantly I remember so many of the great times. Times that no amount of money could replace. I can imagine my mom wanting to give up at times, but she never did. She kept going to work and loving us as she continued to trust that God would make a way out of no way. Although it was hard, she never gave up hope. I truly believe her determination is what kept her going.

She wanted to show us to live in harmony with God and know that we could make it as we work hard and treat everyone with respect. Sometimes, she would talk to you until you were blue in the face, but it was always laughter at the end. Although she had many obstacles to face, she never let us know, or complain about them. She definitely kept it moving. Although she wasn't a strict disciplinarian, she spent a lot of time with us talking. Sometimes you just wanted to say, "Mama, just beat me, please." She talked until she was confident that we got the point she was trying to make. You have to have a want-to mentality because that mentality is a powerful force to be reckoned with. It's one of the most powerful forces on earth. Amazing things can be accomplished with a want-to mentality.

When you really want to get something done, you will do it. There may be difficulties and obstacles, but your determination will get the job done. I have come to the understanding in my own life that I need to stop making lame excuses for things because if I really want to do something, I will do it! I'm convinced I got that from my mom. My mom did what needed to be done without making excuses not to. Can you imagine having to raise ten kids without any help from anyone else? Yes, we got food stamps for a time to help out, but she had to lie on the application about her income in order to get them so one day she made up her mind that she was not going lie any longer and that she was going to have to do it alone and with the help of God, of course, and she did it. Just thinking of raising ten kids alone makes me cringe. I know I can do all things through Christ who strengthens me, but whew, what a job it would be and my mom did it by sheer determination and definitely the grace of God. Mama, I want to tell you, I love you for not giving up and relying on God to make it through. A mother's love is indescribable. I'm reminded of a poem my sister-in-law, Linda Ann sent me:

Highway 109

A drunken man in an Oldsmobile
They said had run a light
That caused the six-car pileup
On 109 that night.

When broken bodies lay about
And blood was everywhere,
The sirens screamed out eulogies,
For death was in the air.

A mother, trapped inside her car,
Was heard above the noise;
Her plaintive plea near split the air:
Oh, God, please spare my boys!
She fought to loose her pinned hands;
She struggled to get free,
But mangled metal held her fast
In grim captivity.

Her frightened eyes then focused
On where the back seat once had been,
But all she saw was broken glass and
Two children's seats crushed in.
Her twins were nowhere to be seen;
She did not hear them cry,
And then she prayed they'd been thrown free,
Oh, God, don't let them die!

Then firemen came and cut her loose,
But when they searched the back,
They found therein no little boys,
But the seat belts were intact.

They thought the woman had gone mad
And was traveling alone,
But when they turned to question her,
They discovered she was gone.

Policemen saw her running wild
And screaming above the noise
In beseeching supplication,
Please help me find my boys!

They're four years old and wear blue shirts;
Their jeans are blue to match.
One cop spoke up, "They're in my car,"
And they don't have a scratch.

They said their daddy put them there
And gave them each a cone,
Then told them both to wait for Mom
To come and take them home.

I've searched the area high and low,
But I can't find their Dad.
He must have fled the scene,
I guess, and that is very bad.

The mother hugged the twins and said,
While wiping at a tear,
He could not flee the scene, you see,
For he's been dead a year.

The cop just looked confused and asked,
Now, how can that be true?
The boys said, Mommy, Daddy came
And left a kiss for you.

He told us not to worry
And that you would be all right,
And then he put us in this car with
The pretty, flashing light.

We wanted him to stay with us,
Because we miss him so,
But Mommy, he just hugged us tight
And said he had to go.

He said someday we'd understand
And told us not to fuss,
And he said to tell you, Mommy,
He's watching over us.

The mother knew without a doubt
That what they spoke was true,
For she recalled their Dad's last words,
I will watch over you.

The firemen's notes could not explain
The twisted, mangled car,
And how the three of them escaped
Without a single scar.
But on the cop's report was scribed,
In print so very fine,
An Angel walked the beat tonight on Highway 109.

—By Ruth Gillis

That mother was determined not to give up and find her kids. Even though she was pinned in, she fought and struggled to get loose to look for her boys. She kept praying as she got up and put some feet to her faith. She knew God heard her prayers and she began looking diligently with passion and persistence for her boys. Nothing or on one was going to stop her. She ran around like a mad tyrant looking and looking for her boys until she found them. Glory to God, when she found them she knew exactly who helped them. She knew it had to be God that kept them. I happened to receive that poem as soon as I was finishing the section about my mom and her determination to survive. God's timing is always perfect. Let that be your attitude toward your dreams. Don't let them die. Continue to pray over them and set goals to reach them until they come to pass. You'll see as the mother in the poem saw that God was watching over them the whole time to keep them alive. The same applies with you as you are determined to not allow circumstances, no matter how hard they are, to kill your determination and drive to accomplish the impossible through Christ. Never give up because of facts. Continue to keep pushing, keep believing the impossible, and keep doing what it takes to press forward. Doing what it takes means getting up and out and putting your hands to the plow to do what God is leading you to do one step at a time. Do not be afraid of the facts not lining up. Do not be afraid of what you see in the natural. God Almighty is your source of support. There will be times when it seems you are alone in your thinking, but do not let that deter you. The enemy will start to play with your mind and say you did not hear from God and you cannot accomplish what God put in you to do, but call him a liar and proceed to victory. People will murmur, complain, and even laugh at you at times, but they did those things to so many other people that accomplished great and wonderful things through Christ. They laughed at Jesus and the disciples. They were all ostracized and criticized by haters. They were mocked, flogged, beaten, spat on along the way, but when God shows you who you are and what you are supposed to be doing here on earth, they can't touch you and they know it. You may even have many false starts, but so what, get back in it and learn from the others and make it happen. Live free of giving up. Live like tomorrow is not promised to you because it's not. Stop putting God off. You will learn as you surrender how blessed you will feel and how fulfilled your heart will be. You will never be happier than literally doing what you were designed to do. It is the ultimate compliment to our Maker. The absolute ultimate way to say, "I appreciate who you created me to be Lord." I love who I am and no one can take that away from me. Now take my advice and go somewhere and let your true identity be revealed by God and see how you will bless so many other people. They will get what God wants them to have from you and so will God. Sometimes, like the mother in the poem, you have to be pushed up against a devastating experience to show the power of God, but make no mistake God is faithful.

I'm also reminded of the story of the renowned pediatric neurosurgeon Ben Carson, who was born to a mother who dropped out of school in the third grade and married when she was only thirteen, but divorced when Ben was only eight. Ben had a brother named Curtis and they were both making bad grades. Ben was called, "Dummy" by the other students by the time he was in the fifth grade. He actually had the worst grades in his class. He was very angry during this time and was displaying an explosive temper. His mom knew she had to help her sons. She began to pray persistently that she would have the wisdom about what she should do that would help Ben and Curtis to learn what they needed to learn for them to do well in school. She started disciplining their time at home by limiting their television time, not allowing them to play until schoolwork was completed, and also encouraging them to read two books per week and do reports on them both. This yielded great results. Ben, as a result realized that he was not "dumb" and could learn as well as anyone else. He was also able to control his temper and get along with the other students. Ben completed high school with honors and went to college at Yale University where he obtained a degree in Psychology. He was preparing to be a psychiatrist, but once he got to medical school, at the University of Michigan, he changed his mind and pursued neurosurgery instead. He completed his residency at one of the most prestigious hospitals in the world, Johns Hopkins in Baltimore, Maryland. He went on to become director of pediatric neurosurgery by the time he was in his thirties and he happened also to be the youngest person to ever hold such a position at that hospital. To date, he remains in the position and is a professor of neurological surgery, oncology, plastic surgery, and pediatrics at Johns Hopkins medical school. He is also called upon for speaking engagements to encourage young people about how they can fulfill their intellectual potential.

When you are faced with obstacles, do not allow them to be stopping blocks. Take them for what they are, just obstacles. Jump over them, hurl over them, step over them, or step on top of them, but do what it takes not to give up. They do not have to stop you if you don't want them to. As you pursue the things you want to conquer, if you want them bad enough, you will achieve them. You will also start to discover other things along the way that you happen to be good at doing and enjoy doing. You will find out more about yourself through obstacles than any other thing in your life. There will be things that will amuse you, but also things that will surprise you about yourself that will be used to enable you to be better at what you dream to do. There is a path of discovery that you should apply yourself to obtain and then use to complete your dreams. Everything about you is complimentary to your dreams in order that you will be able to reach them. That's why it's important to know yourself and the God who created you. In times of challenge and discouragement you need to be able to talk yourself up and say what God says about you. Can you imagine the amount of people who just gave up on their children and took what people said about them to heart without consulting God the way Ben Carson's mother did. When we ask God he will show us more than we could ever imagine on our own. When we depend on God He will help us to achieve more than we could ever imagine. We will grow into that person that God is obliged to help as we discover our treasure. Then we are in pursuit of what God wants for us and are then living in harmony with what God has designed for us to become.

I'm still learning more and more about myself. Some good and some bad, but rest assured, it will all be used to help me dig out more and more of my valuable treasure. Never be discouraged about the shortcomings that you discover about yourself. Just make the correction and know that God is helping you to familiarize you with yourself so that you can be aware of areas that need prayer in your life. My shortcomings keep me in prayer in my own life and keep me humble and teachable. They also keep me totally dependent on God because they remind me that I cannot accomplish God's will on my own. They keep me humble enough to ask for help even when I don't think I need it. We don't have to know everything because God does and we have His help as soon as we call on Him. I am constantly growing as I learn more about myself and agree with God on how to fix it. I also found that for me, apologies are a way I show myself and God that I agree with His way of doing things and not my own. When we apologize to people, we are correcting some things within ourselves that God has shown us and by submitting to God as well as submitting ourselves to those individuals for their forgiveness. We should always be sensitive enough to learn what we need to be aware of about ourselves, in order to maximize our potential. God will make even your flaws turn around for your good. How powerful is that? What an amazing love the Father has for us. Always continue to remind yourself of that powerful truth. It will strengthen and encourage you in the most difficult times. It will help you breathe when the breath gets knocked out of you. It will pick you up when you are at your lowest. It will shake you back to believing every promise He has told you to stand on. It will give you great peace of mind as you continue on in Him. Take the time to just think on God's love and become persuaded of it. That will fill you up with whatever you need.

Romans 8:35-38 says:

> "Who shall separate us from the love of Christ? Shall tribulation, or distress, or persecution, or famine, or nakedness, or peril, or sword? As it is written: For Your sake we are killed all day long; We are accounted as sheep for the slaughter. Yet in all these things we are more than conquerors through Him who loved us. For I am persuaded that neither death not life, or angels, nor principalities, nor powers, nor things present, nor things to come, nor height, nor depth, nor any other created thing, shall be able to separate me from the love of God which is in Christ Jesus our Lord."

Listen, people can chop us up however they please, but when we meditate on that love, and our treasure becomes more and more prevalent as we engage in intimate time with Him, all of their efforts are in vain. He then becomes the object of our attention and affection. We begin to live to please Him. He responds to us by showing us great things about ourselves. He shows us this great treasure that He has given us so we can use it to glorify Him that the excellence may be of Him. It's an extraordinary transference of power and purpose that we obtain from the Father.

CHAPTER 7

TREASURE ACTIVATED THROUGH INTIMACY WITH GOD

Lets discuss intimacy. We have to understand that intimacy has to take place between us and the Father in order to truly discover our hidden treasure because He is the only one that knows it fully in order to reveal it to us. When we become intimate with God, we become impregnated with purpose. We are taken on a journey with God to reveal our treasure in bits and pieces. He gives us dreams and visions of ourselves being used mightily by Him. It is beyond our ability to even fathom; therefore, we sometimes shun it off or just brush it off as being some fantasy. But then, we begin to see it more and more as we become closer to Him and it just won't go away. It grows within us as we encounter Him and pursue Him. We then understand that it has been God all along and not just our imagination. Conception has occurred within us from intimacy with God. In order to be intimate with the Father, you have to get to know Him. You have to spend time with Him in order to get to know Him. That not only enhances your confidence level, but it also allows what it truly takes for God to gain unhindered access to your will and transform it into His will. This is a process that many try to avoid because it entails giving up so much of yourself or should I say it entails so much dying on your part. I remember not wanting to get close to God because I was so afraid of what I would have to give up or what people would say about me. Maybe they would say some of the things I said about others when they sold out to God and surrendered their lives wholly to Him. I am guilty myself, of saying a thing or two about holy rollers. Now, I am one myself and am proud of it. I admit I am a holy roller and I thank God for it. I thank God He looked over my ignorance and saw my need. I am so grateful that He didn't hold my actions against Him, or against me. If I only knew then, what I know now. If I had really taken the time to stop and give His love a chance. That's all He was trying to do. He was just trying to get His true love to me and I rejected it because of selfish ambition. I didn't understand that He had much more for me than anything I could ever achieve on my own. I really look back now and give God thanks for His grace and mercy. He kept me until I decided I'd turn to Him with my whole heart. You may be reading this book and wondering how you can obtain a personal relationship and experience intimacy with the Father. It's easy. All you have to do is draw near to Him. Hebrews 10:22 says, "*Let us all come forward and draw near with true (honest and sincere) hearts in unqualified assurance and absolute conviction engendered by human personality on God in absolute trust and confidence in His power, wisdom, and goodness), having our hearts sprinkled and purified from a guilty (evil) conscience and our bodies cleansed with pure water.*" This is how you gain access as a believer. Do not pursue your treasure and not pursue Him. It doesn't work that way. Pursue God and your treasure will be revealed. Remember God is the most important part of your treasure. Your treasure will show how powerful God is in your life. Just draw near to Him with your whole heart and continue to seek Him. Be consistent in your pursuit of His presence. Be persistent and diligent and He will do the rest, I promise. Continue to do it on a daily basis. The more you draw near to Him, the more He will lead and guide you and you will know it's Him. Intimacy with our Father is the best thing that ever happened to me. I found my true self in that intimacy. I found more out about Him and His love for me. He gave me confidence in myself. I have become comfortable in my skin, no matter whose company I am in. I see things with a different set of eyes. I hear things with a different set of ears. My perspective used to be negative, but by the grace of God, He has shown me how better to look at things that happen. He has shown me that there is the world's perspective and there is God's perspective. I must admit, I thought like the world and still do in some instances until God shows me His perspective on a matter and that does it for me now. It does not have to be proven for me to believe it. I just do because I trust Him. I trust Him because He has shown himself faithful over and over again. I can go on and on about me and Him, but I'll just stop right there. I am getting chills just thinking and writing of our intimacy. Oh, how I love Him.

There is no getting pass intimacy with God and discovering your treasure. It is absolutely impossible and I'm so glad because it has truly enriched my life in countless ways. Your treasure is meant to be revealed to you on a personal level by God. God gave it to you and it is going to take Him to reveal it to you. Along the way, you will experience God in so many fascinating ways. Hebrews 11:6b says:

"For whoever would come near to God must [necessarily] believe that God exists and that He is the rewarder of those who earnestly and diligently seek Him."

Whatever we do for God should be a result of the fact that we love Him, not because we try to get something from Him. Just think of that, we get to know Him and we get rewarded for it. I know I have diligently sought the Lord, although in the past I was treating Him like a part time lover, but no more. I made up my mind to diligently seek Him with all my heart. That means that I qualify for rewards. I may not deserve the blessings, but I receive all the blessings that He decides to give me and you should do the same.

Intimacy will enrich, empower, enlighten, and enhance you. I like to think of it as the "wow" moments in life where God shows you Himself in profound ways. He will show you so many aspects to His true character. This will be one of the most memorable experiences that you will ever have in life. Truly surrender yourself to Him. You will always remember when you truly surrendered. God is waiting for that moment from all of us. It is so freeing to surrender. It takes everything off of you and puts it on Him and with open arms He takes it all. That's what He wants. He wants it all. God wants to be your every thing. He doesn't want anything withheld from Him. I have to stop here and pause because I am just thinking on His wonderful grace and perfect love towards us. It compels me to want to love Him and be used by Him more and more. I want to stir your gift/gifts up as well. Be that one who will step out on faith and not turn back. Begin to believe in yourself the way God wants you to. You have a lot to offer. You can begin right where you are as you get connected to God. That connection will have you to start right where you are and take one step at a time. I'm discovering more and more of my treasure, but now that I am confident that I have something valuable for the Kingdom of God, I'm more pressed to not only discover all of it, but to spend it all up for the Kingdom. I know that mankind awaits my contribution to it. I have special designed abilities given to me at my origin to make a difference in this world for the Kingdom of God. I am surely blessed to be a part of God's purpose to save as many souls as I can by using all that has been given me to use. You are great in the Kingdom of God. You have greatness inside of you ready to be revealed. You can conquer anything God places at your fingertips to do. You are treasured with treasure to be used for Kingdom purposes. That is not to be taken lightly. Don't limit your capabilities by thinking you do not have something great inside of you. Everyone has this treasure inside to be revealed that it may glorify God and add to the Kingdom of God. You are well equipped to do great things. Never feel inadequate because God knows exactly what you have and as you surrender it all to Him, He will use it as He sees fit. That is the beauty about it. It's so valuable that the enemy hates it when you are completely surrendered. God is quite aware of that and you must be as well. The enemy will try to stop you, frustrate you, discourage you, distract you, persecute you, and condemn you out of completing your earthly assignment, but 2 Corinthians 2:11 says:

"Lest Satan should get an advantage of us:
for we are not ignorant of his devices."

Please do not allow those things to deter you. You never know how God is going to use you at any given moment when you are surrendered. It's exciting being used by God to save lives and change the course of the lives of real human beings. It is very rewarding as well. It satisfies the greatest hunger inside you. You are at peace with yourself and completely convinced that you are valuable and no one can take that away from you, especially not Satan. He becomes insignificant in the grand scheme of things because you begin to see the power of God destroy anything Satan tries to do to you to stop you. Blessed assurance, Jesus is mine. Glory to God! We have the power of Almighty God on our side.

When I think of the power of God and all the promises He has given us to help us as we complete His purpose, Psalms 91 comes to mind. Psalms 91 is absolutely remarkable and will keep us grounded with the power of God that we have at our disposal. In every situation, He is there. I don't know about you, but sometimes I feel like I'm the only one that can really see what's happening and that I'm alone, but that could not be farther from the truth. In fact, God is all over it. I just have to acknowledge Him so He can direct me through it. He has our answer and He hears our cry, whether it is a silent cry on the inside or one that is loud and is heard. Lets take a look at Psalm 91, in its entirety, one scripture at a time. It will bless you as it does me every time I study and meditate on it. Take one scripture at a time and just let it resonate in your spirit. I'm sure you will find yourself in it. It is designed to capture the very heart of what you are experiencing. Take it and personalize it in a prayer for yourself. Even if it's just one of them that pertains to you at this moment, use it to meditate on and hear what God has to say to you. See won't He comfort and reassure you in the most amazing way as only He can do. You will find that even though you may have many that will want to help and attempt to help, sometimes you just need to get alone with God about it and let Him minister to your spirit.

Psalms 91:1-16

"1. He who dwells in the secret place of the Most High
Shall abide under the shadow of the Almighty.
2. I will say of the Lord, "He is my refuge and
my fortress; My God, in Him I will trust."
3. Surely He shall deliver you from the snare of
the fowler and from the perilous pestilence.
4. He shall cover you with His feathers, and
under His wings you shall take refuge; His
truth shall be your shield and buckler.
5. You shall not be afraid of the terror by
night, nor of the arrow that flies by day,
6. nor of the pestilence that walks in darkness, nor
of the destruction that lays waste at noonday.
7. A thousand may fall at your side, and ten thousand
at your right hand; But it shall not come near you.
8. Only with your eyes shall you look,
and see the reward of the wicked.
9. Because you have made the Lord, Who is my
refuge, even the Most High, your dwelling place,
10. No evil shall befall you, nor shall any
plague come near your dwelling;
11. For He shall give His angels charge over
you, to keep you in all your ways.
12. In their hands they shall bear you up,
lest you dash your foot against a stone.
13. You shall tread upon the lion and the cobra, the young
lion and the serpent, you shall trample underfoot.
14. Because he has set his love upon me, therefore I will deliver
him; I will set him on high, because he has known My name.
15. He shall call upon Me, and I will answer him; I will be
with him in trouble; I will deliver him and honor him.
16. With long life I will satisfy him,
and show him My salvation. "

Glory to God! That really comforts me. I'm elated to know that God has us covered, no matter what the enemy tries to do. Satan is a defeated foe. He has no power over the power of God in your life so get up, gear up and go get them tiger. You have places to go in Christ, people to see in Christ, and things to do for the Kingdom of God. God is faithful and will deliver you out of trouble when it comes to hinder you. You can be secure in Him when you pursue purpose. You can have peace of mind that He is definitely there for you to call upon at any given moment and He will be there for you. He will also reward you for what you do out of a pure heart. Jeremiah 17:10 says:

"I the Lord search the mind, I try the heart,
even to give to every man according to his ways,
according to the fruit of his doings."

When your motives are correct, God will reward you. The scripture says, "according to your ways, according to the fruit of your doings." That is saying God is aware of why you do it and the fruit that comes out of it and you will be rewarded. Now lets look at it another way. If your motives are incorrect you will still be rewarded according to your ways and according to the fruit of your doings. So be careful that you are being led by God to do what you do so you can be rewarded with a good reward. Examine yourself, what are your motives? What are the fruit of what you do?

God's reward system is like no other. I had to come to the realization that because I can be selfish at times, I truly need to examine my motives so I can be in God's will and not my own. I want my motives to be right. I want to have a pure heart before the Lord when I do things for the Kingdom. Be honest with yourself and take a self- examination of your motives as well. It will bless you and cleanse you at the same time. I love it when I can see correction in my behavior. It tells me that God is really working on me as I often ask Him to do. It also shows me that He cares for me dearly because He chastens those He loves. Even though it does not feel good at the time, I try my best to hear and heed the leading of the Holy Spirit. Hebrews 12:11 says:

"Now no chastening for the present seems to be joyous, but grievous: nevertheless afterward it yields the peaceable fruit of righteousness unto them which are exercised thereby."

God chastens us so that He can get us to yield the fruit of righteousness because we are the righteousness of God in Christ Jesus; therefore we should be yielding righteous fruit. I look at it as cultivating for a better harvest. We are the righteousness of God in Christ, so we should be yielding righteous fruit. We should be sowing seeds of righteousness that will bring forth fruit to glorify God.

I believe you are going to do great exploits for the Kingdom of God. I believe God is showing you even now what your treasure is and you are going to start right where you are to use it. You are already familiar with what you do well. Start there and let God show you more about yourself. Start to daily get in your word to get a closer walk with God and get to know His thoughts and ways. It will be the best thing that ever happened to you. A relationship with God the Father is not one you want to miss. I have experienced many relationships, but there is none that could even compare to having one with God. He will somehow help your heart feel absolutely secure in the most trying circumstances. As you get to know Him, He will begin to transform your thinking and renew your mind with the word of God. I love God, I love people, and I love myself now and because of my relationship with God, He got me to the point of allowing and yielding to His will to let that love flourish for His glory. Miracles signs and wonders can happen in that type of atmosphere, where love is prevalent and God is in control. God is the God of miracles. He is very aware of our shortcomings and He will be our strength, but we have to trust Him to step out and trust His will for our lives. Philippians 2:13 says:

"It is He that works in us both to will and to do for His good pleasure."

God uses His love for us and ours for Him to work on our hearts that we will yield to His will that His purpose may prevail. I can almost pinpoint the time I really surrendered to Gods will. It was both scary and satisfying. This awesome peace just flooded my body and spirit and I have not been the same since. I understand being all tangled up in Jesus. I never want to leave His presence and I want to continue to do His will. There are blessings in doing His will. The word is His will and as you receive His word completely, you will see His will clearly through it. Your treasure depends on you to be able to rightly divide the word of God so you can administer your treasure appropriately. You want the excellence to always be of God and not of yourself. Yes, you should be admired for allowing God to use you, but draw the line when it comes to allowing people to skip God's hand in your life. God's grace is so amazing. It will be right there every time to invade you with the ability to do the work so you can abound, not just get by, but abound in every good work. I get so stirred up when I think of the grace of God because many people will look at you when you tell them about what God has shown you to do with wonder, thinking to themselves now how are you going to do that. By the grace of God, that's how. I really love God's grace because sometimes I can't even explain how I can do what I do, but when I reflect on the grace to God, I realize it's His abounding grace that shows up for me and I am humbled and so grateful to God. When we pray for help, God's grace shows up as our aid to help in time of need. Hebrews 4:16 says:

"Let us therefore come boldly unto the throne of grace, that we may obtain mercy, and find grace to help in time of need."

Whatever the need is, His grace is sufficient. When the need is great, His grace abounds. When the need is somewhat small, His grace still abounds. What is so special about the grace of God is that it is designed to abound for every good work. Small or great, grace steps up to the plate and abounds on your behalf. Take grace and live according to the knowledge that it will show up at the right time. When you come to a place that seems overwhelming please know that God is never overwhelmed. His grace is in place for you at any given moment.

Your treasure will be the very thing that you can always rely on to bring you that satisfaction in knowing that you are doing what you were created to do. When you are using your treasure, it will come and provide that divine inner peace that will override all the insecurity that comes along with being out of the will of God. You will have and inner sense of peace that will keep you driven beyond the normal person pursuing worldly things. You will be talked about. It won't stop you. Your life will be under a microscope. It won't matter. You will lose friends. You will realize their true colors. You will feel lonely at times, but you will know the timing is right for you to do what you were created to do. You will completely be convinced of who you are. You will be able to deal with offense better than ever before because you will know why it's coming. No matter the situation, you will know God's purpose will prevail. In all we do as we embark on really being who God created us to be, we have to realize that it has a season. Ecclesiastes 3:1 says:

> *"To every thing there is a season, and a time*
> *to every purpose under the heaven."*

Your treasure is to be used at an appointed time for the purpose God created it. There is a time for every purpose. Use what has been given you at each appointed time afforded to you. When a door opens to use your treasure for the kingdom of God, by all means seize that moment and capitalize on it for the sake of the kingdom of God that God's purpose will prevail. There may be times in your life that are very hard to get through, but even in those times you can use your treasure to allow God to bring about purpose.

Do not allow tough times to stifle you. I have been stifled before because of tough times and distractions and have missed what God had for me to do. God showed me how I missed it. Not to condemn, but to convict me enough to be able to see His purpose is more important than my feelings. I know that may sound like God is cold, but the very opposite is true. God will use that to align my feelings up to what is really important. I had to begin to put my feelings in proper perspective when it came to doing the will of God. Your feelings will be used by the enemy to stop the plan of God, if you do not put them under the subjection of the word of God. Many times my feelings were a detour that I should not have taken. I know for sure of blessings I missed because of my feelings. I also know how I could have been a blessing to others, but was stopped by my feelings. I had to start looking at it as if a life was at stake every time I followed my feelings instead of the will of God. Positive confession is the vehicle God used with me to get my feeling out of the way of divine purpose. I had allowed my feelings to oppress me. When I realized what was happening, I quickly gave it to God and asked for help with my feelings. They will no longer get in the way of my treasure being used for the purpose God created me. I talked my way into doing many things that yielded Godly results for the kingdom. Instead of talking myself "out" of doing it, I talked my way "into" doing His will.

The word says, "We can do all things through Christ who strengthens us." Over and over again, I have used that scripture to counter my wrong feelings and you must do the same. Do not allow you feelings to move you out of the will of God. It took me such a long time to discover that our feelings are used by the enemy to keep us in bondage and play tricks on you to make you go in the direction they want you to go, which is usually contrary to the will of God. 1 Corinthians 15:58 says:

"Therefore, my beloved brethren, be firm (steadfast), immoveable, always abounding in the work of the Lord [always being superior, excelling, doing more than enough in the service of the Lord], knowing and being continually aware that your labor in the Lord is not futile [it is never wasted or to no purpose]."

Notice it said, "always abounding in the work of the Lord" and as I quoted earlier about God's grace abounding towards us. God's grace will be that abounding power for your work in the Lord. Just begin to pray for God's grace to show up in hard times. The scripture also stated that your labor in the Lord is never futile or never wasted or to no purpose. Your labor in the Lord is God's purpose prevailing here on earth. Your labor is not in vain. God is using everything you do for Him to enhance the Kingdom of God. You are on God's clock and you serve an eternal purpose. Our treasure serves eternal purposes. These purposes are so unique that no two of us are absolutely identical. Our unique purpose is why it is so remarkable how God orchestrates our treasure. When God sees you, He sees greatness waiting to happen. He created you with powerful potential to change the world around you. We all have been given grace to help us as we walk by faith. Ephesians 4:7 says:

> *"But to every one of us is given grace according*
> *to the measure of the gift of Christ."*

The grace of God is given to us to use our treasure that God gives us. It is given according to the measure of our gift or treasure to be used for the kingdom. That makes His grace sufficient for you. God never expects us to do it alone.

He expects us to need Him and call on Him. That's why the excellence of the power will be of Him and not of us. Many times I say with a sigh of relief, "If it weren't for the grace of God." I want to stir you up on the inside and let you see your amazing abilities in Him. Remember, you are a treasure and the treasure you have inside of you is waiting to be unleashed from within you for the glory of God. Don't stop when it gets hard. Stand firm on your assignment and see it through. You may have many false starts, but never give up on it. God is counting on us to win souls to the Kingdom but we can't by giving up. God will send you help if needed. Encouragement from someone who has been through is priceless. That's why we need to continue to encourage one another as we recognize the same struggles others go through that we have made it through. You will find that when you encourage others, you will be encouraged as well because as you share your experiences, you will get to remember how God brought you through some of the same situations they are going through and be reminded that if He did it then, He can do it again. Although you may be going through something else, it will remind you of His power to bring you through that as well. I love encouraging others. I love seeing others get breakthroughs. It really blesses me because it reminds me of Gods great love for us. I want to be instrumental in helping others get their breakthroughs.

Whether it is with finances, advice, prayer, training, teaching, or my books, I want to help people. I love people and I enjoy helping them. When you understand how passionate God is about that, you will feel the same way. In fact, I think there are people who are reading this book that have discovered they feel the same way. Acts 21:35 says:

> *"In everything I have pointed out to you [by example] that, by working diligently in this manner, we ought to assist the weak, being mindful of the words of the Lord Jesus, how He, Himself, said, It is more blessed (makes one happier and more to be envied) to give than to receive."*

So move the enemy out of your way and do it. It's never to late. Start today doing something small for someone and see won't it bless you. It's not you taking God's glory, but it's God in you saying, "Well done, my good and faithful servant." God will then put a longing in your heart to do more for people to save them and help them. God will begin to allow you to see yourself in amazing ways. Nothing you could even imagine doing on your own. You will have to be totally dependent on Him to accomplish His will.

You cannot be worried about being embarrassed because there will be plenty of times that God will ask you to do or say something to someone to help them that may embarrass you, especially if they are not receptive to what you are saying or doing. That to me, is one of the hardest to get use to, but in time when you see the results and people helped and lives being changed because of that one act of obedience, you will want to obey even more. Notice I didn't say you will be more comfortable, but you will want to obey more because God wants His will done no matter your comfort level because you will have to sacrifice other things in order to accomplish what you are put here to do; however, you won't feel like you are missing something. Instead, you will feel completely fulfilled because you are doing what you are supposed to do. Your treasure is inside of you to be used for that function. Your treasure is uniquely you. It will distinguish you from the crowd and obtain Godly results.

There are countless people in the world who are dissatisfied with their lives and experiencing feelings of being unfulfilled due to not doing what they are meant to do. When you find your treasure, you have to be diligent to do it. You have to give yourself to what you are meant to do. By that I mean, God has given us our treasure to use not to just let it lay dormant. We should nourish and develop it. Find out what your treasure is and give yourself to it. Don't half step. Go all the way. Now, there are things that we may want to do, but have not been given the ability to do it. For example, I would love to play the piano. My husband tried to teach me, but we quickly learned that was not what I was talented to do. I was basically wasting precious time that I could have been using on what I really am meant to do. We cannot accomplish something great just because we want to do it. God only helps us do what He wants us to do.

Only God has the ability to really use your treasure properly. Only God is meant to use your treasure for His glory. Only God will pull from your treasure at the proper time. Only God has the ability to know when He needs what out of you. All of your treasure will not manifest at once, that's why we have to surrender to God and let Him withdraw from what He has intricately placed in us, little by little and piece by piece, until His glory is revealed and others have experienced God through you so they may be helped, healed, set free, or delivered. As 2 Timothy 4:5 says:

"But you be watchful in all things, endure afflictions, do the work of and evangelist, fulfill your ministry."

MANNA-FEST DESTINY MINISTRIES

To equip the saints to uplift God and spread the 'Good News' about Jesus Christ, the abundant life He came to give, by the life we live and the service we give. We are and will become living bibles for the world to read. We are hereto provoke change in our lives, the lives of our families, our communities, and our world. We are lights to the world that will not be hidden. We see no limitsin God as we embark into the possible to affect the impossible. We come to build, claim, and provoke the manifestation of what God has already given us.

Hours of Service:

Manna-Fest Destiny Ministries, Dixon:
Sunday Service - 8:30AM
Corporate Prayer - 7PM

Manna-Fest Destiny Ministries, Dixon:
Sunday Service - 11AM
Wednesday Night Bible Study - 7PM

Note from the Publisher

Are you a first time author?

Not sure how to proceed to get your book published?
Want to keep all your rights and all your royalties?
Want it to look as good as a Top 10 publisher?
Need help with editing, layout, cover design?
Want it out there selling in 90 days or less?

Visit our website for some exciting new options!

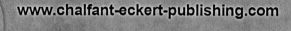

www.chalfant-eckert-publishing.com

CPSIA information can be obtained
at www.ICGtesting.com
Printed in the USA
FFOW05n0314180116

9 781633 081895